SELF BELIEF:
THE VISION

SELF BELIEF:
THE VISION

How to Be a Success on Your Own Terms

JAMAL
EDWARDS

2 4 6 8 10 9 7 5 3 1

First published in the UK in 2013 by Virgin Books,
an imprint of Ebury Publishing
A Random House Group Company

Writer/researcher: Wendy Roby
Commissioning editor: Hannah Knowles
Publishing strategy: Crystal Mahey-Morgan

The Random House Group Limited Reg. No. 954009

Addresses for companies within the Random House Group can be
found at www.randomhouse.co.uk

A CIP catalogue record for this book is available from
the British Library

The Random House Group Limited supports The Forest Stewardship
Council (FSC®), the leading international forest certification
organisation. All our titles that are printed on Greenpeace-approved
FSC®-certified paper carry the FSC® logo. Our paper procurement
policy can be found at www.randomhouse.co.uk/environment

Typeset by e-type
Printed and bound by CPI Group (UK) Ltd, Croydon, CR0 4YY

ISBN 9780753555392

To buy books by your favourite authors and register for offers visit
www.randomhouse.co.uk

CONTENTS

TAKE CONTROL

Level 1

FOREWORD

When people ask me what an entrepreneur is, my answer is someone who wants to make a difference to other people's lives. Jamal is a walking definition of the word. He started out with an idea, and has used that idea to bring his passion for music to his generation.

When Jamal entered the Virgin Media Pioneer competition in 2011, he asked how I would develop a youth channel such as SB.TV into an organisation as successful as mine. Jamal's a bright guy, with enough energy to fuel a rocket, but he understood the importance of looking for, and listening to, advice from someone who's achieved in a similar field.

Like Jamal, I started out in business as a teenager, with *Student* magazine and then Virgin Records. I had so many raw ideas and ambition – the hardest thing was working out how to make those ideas become real, existing ventures. In *Self Belief: The Vision*, Jamal shares his experiences – good and bad – and passes on his advice in typically innovative and interactive fashion.

Get yourself involved in Jamal's challenges to help make your vision a reality, and maybe it's you I'll be seeing as one of Virgin Media's Pioneers of the future...

Sir Richard Branson, 2013

TAKE CONTROL

INTRO

Wassup! Jamal here. Thanks for buying *Self Belief: The Vision*. It's cool you've decided to join me.

I've written this book because I want other people like me to have the confidence to turn their dream into a reality. When I was fifteen and filming foxes with my camera, I had no idea I was going to end up meeting people like Dr Dre, or running my own record label. It's not like I was reading accounting manuals in my nappies or freaking out over spreadsheets when I was in primary school. I mean, I had no idea how to build a media company when I started making videos; I just had a vision and the determination to have a go and try to see it through.

Sometimes all it takes is for one person to give you permission to have a go at pursuing your ideas – whether you want to start your own fashion brand, set up a bar, write a book, or maybe just get your voice heard at work or in your community. I want to try to be that person for anyone who reads this book. I want to encourage you to get out of bed and try things, and switch it up a bit. Don't stay in bed unless you can make money from your bed. And not like *that*, either!

Some of these levels will tell the story of SB.TV and how I went from being a kid from West London who worked weekends at Topman to running a media business full time. I'm not telling you my story because I want to impress you, but I do want to see if there's anything you can learn from the things I think I did right. I made a few mistakes along the way, so it'd be cool if someone could learn from those too :)

How does this work?

The levels of *Self Belief: The Vision* are designed to make you figure out where your own personal talents lie, improve your confidence and understand how to approach problems, in the hope that the path towards your goal is easier than it might have been. I'm going to set you challenges to complete; I'm going to give you all the tips I wish I'd known before I got started; I'm also gonna give you some tasks to try, to see if it makes you think differently about yourself. I want to hear how it's going as you do them – so tweet me @selfbelievers, let me know what your vision is and what you're doing to get there. It doesn't matter what your idea is, or if you just want to increase your confidence. But it'd be cool if some of you can turn the thing you love into the thing you *do*. Like I did.

The other thing about *Self Belief: The Vision* is you don't just *read* it. You have to choose your own path within it, and there'll be forks in the road now and again where you can choose to go down one route or another. Each time you make a choice at a Decision Point, you'll go down a new path. There are no right or wrong answers. It's a game; except it's not.

This first level is about taking control. I wanted to start here because a lot of people think that the key qualities that successful people or entrepreneurs share are confidence, risk-taking and having guts. Maybe that's what I had, and I just didn't realise. So I want to get you away from thinking 'Why are things not happening for me?' to a point where you're in charge of your own destiny.

Let's go...

MY STORY

Life lessons

When I was young, I had so much energy, I was bouncing off the walls. My mum was smart though, because she put me in stage school on Saturdays to tire me out. We did performances of *Oliver*, *Cats* and *Annie*, things like that – it was so jokes. I was a force of nature but my mum knew it made sense to keep me occupied so that when I came home from stage school, I'd just collapse. Which meant that when there was sometimes trouble on the estate, I wasn't around to be involved in it.

That's not to say I didn't get into trouble. On my estate we were always messing about, but it was mainly just low-level stuff. There were abandoned cars on our estate, so we used to break open the cars. I don't know if that was normal stuff for a young kid to be doing, but it was normal where I lived, so I just joined in because it was what everyone was doing. It was dumb but it was exciting at the time; you do feel kind of alive when you've got to run away after throwing a rock.

Then something terrible happened and I knew I had to grow out of it. I was about fourteen and it was the last day of school. We were all mucking about and someone sprayed deodorant in my face and I just kicked off. I literally flipped. I took a chair and smashed it in his face. The next thing I knew a police car drew up in the playground and I was being arrested and taken away in it, while everyone was staring at me. And then I was sitting in a cell, waiting, and the guy I'd hit was in hospital and I didn't know if he was going to make it or not. It was bad.

When I was sitting in the cell, I was like, 'Oh. My. Days.' I had to wear this white suit because they took away all my clothes. I just thought, 'Am I really doing this?' They told me I could choose between three solicitors to represent me and at that point I knew I had to phone my mum and tell her what I'd done. That was the turning point for me, that was when I realised I needed to fix up and look at myself: I didn't want this to be me. My mum was so upset with me, she was saying, 'Jamal, why you doing this?' I could tell she was really disappointed, even though she was calming and comforting on the phone. That was a wake-up thing for me, that was big.

So after that I kept things in check, and tried to stay focused. Some people think that you have to be born an entrepreneur – like, you need to arrive with this crazy, money-making gene that most people aren't born with. I'm not sure that's true. But I was certainly always looking for opportunities.

Always looking for an angle

When everyone was collecting Merlin Premier League football stickers at school, I was trying to find an angle. I used to sell my spares because there was this craze for collecting. I used to buy a pack every day from the post office on the way home and see if I could get any of the shiny stickers, because they were the best ones. And then I'd go round all my friends and see if I had stickers anyone else needed. But I didn't just sell to the first person who wanted them, I would check with *everyone*, so I could get the highest price for each sticker. You could get a pound for just one sticker, so it became kind of addictive; being the guy everyone would come to for stickers.

THINGS TO THINK ABOUT

That might sound silly when I'm talking about selling stickers and figuring out how to get the best deal, but it *is* something you have to think about when you're trying to get something off the ground. Do your research. If you've got an idea for a business or activity that you think will improve people's lives, you need to find out first who wants the thing you have, and how much they're willing to pay for it. I was just a kid, but I knew if there were ten people who were collecting the Merlins, I would need to check with every one of them before I sold my swaps. And I've still got that sticker book, man, and even though it's all Sellotaped together and it's been through *the wars,* it reminds me of when I was young and how I got started.

I know not everyone will think like me. Some of you may be great at planning and amazing at organising yourselves, whereas I've got like, 48K unread emails. So before you set out to make your vision happen, you need to fix up and look at yourself to see what areas of your life, character or skills you need to work on in order to be successful. Because even if you've spotted a gap in the market, had an idea for a business or already decided that you want to start a campaigning group in your community, you'll need to be confident, brave and unafraid of risks to really make it happen.

Are you already confident enough to approach strangers with an idea and get them excited about it? Do you feel good about the skills you bring to the table? Could you send fifty emails in a day to people who you want to be part of your vision? It doesn't matter if you can't, but it's important to know yourself *before* you begin. And be honest.

THE CHALLENGE

To get you thinking about YOU, this first challenge is about taking a step back. I want you to look at yourself to see if you can identify what you need to work on. Instead of always hanging around in the same park or club or shopping centre, or talking to the same people, watching the same things or playing the same video games, this week you're gonna switch it up. Partly to help you realise just how much you're capable of, and partly so you can work out what areas you might need help with.

What are you like?

First off, let's imagine you're in a new college or a new office for the day. You don't know anyone; you don't know what part of the building you're supposed to be in; you don't know how things work. Maybe you notice stuff before other people do. You're someone who watches rather than gets involved right away – the kind of person who finds rooms full of people chatting really loud kind of intimidating. Or maybe you're excited to see what the girls/guys in that college/office look like, or what kind of music everyone's into, or where they got their clothes. Really picture it and try to imagine your reaction. Are you nervous? Or can you not wait to get stuck in?

Making connections

When I used to work near Oxford Circus in central London, the shop I worked in was quite near Portland Place, which is where some of the BBC offices are based. At the end of my shift, I would head to the bus stop to go home, or out with my mates, or to film something for SB.TV. But instead of walking the logical, quickest way from the shop to the Tube station, I would go the long way round, past the BBC offices. I did that because I was curious to see who I might pass on the street. Maybe someone would have been visiting Radio 1 for an interview, or maybe there were people working on a music show, or celebrities who'd been on a TV programme. I also knew that if I deliberately took the long way round enough times, I'd start recognising people who maybe weren't famous, but who worked at the BBC. And since I'd already decided I wanted to work in the media, those people seemed like good people to get to know.

The first time I clocked someone from the BBC (sometimes they wear security passes), I'd smile at them as I walked past. Maybe they'd just think I was being polite, or was in a good mood – I wasn't really worried about what they thought of me at that point.

So the first few times I saw them, I'd smile again. Then the next five times, I'd maybe just say 'Hi' and see if they said 'Hi' back. The point is, once you've said 'Hi' ten times to a complete stranger, it feels weird for them (or you) not to make that interaction last a little bit longer. They might assume you do know them, or that they have met you once, but they've forgotten. Again, it doesn't matter. Because eventually it went from 'Hi!' to 'How's it going?' to 'What's your name again?' and then there'd be that one, golden day when they'd say, 'Hey Jamal, how's it going?' and they'd know my name.

That probably sounds like a really small thing that wouldn't get you anywhere, but it's making connections with people that gets your self-belief right up, and helps you get places. So I want you to give it a go...

- If there's somewhere you've always wanted to work, or love seeing gigs at, go out of your way to walk past it. Maybe you can do a detour on your way to or from college or to work – that's a great time of day to see people who work at the places you want to be at.

- Start off noticing the people you pass each day. Maybe there are people you see more than once.

- Give them a smile – not in a weird way, just being friendly as you pass. Then if you see them again, say hello.

- After a while of doing this, and it might take a few weeks rather than days, you'll start to recognise people and they'll recognise you. Maybe you can start a chat with them. Don't force it though – you don't want to bug people by making them talk to you if they don't want to!

If you get that interaction a few times, you've got them hooked, and you've got a new contact, a new person to help you achieve your vision. That's one way I used to get to know people at the BBC, and eventually managed to swing a work experience placement there. Just by taking a different route to the bus stop.

DECISION POINT

Throughout each level of *Self Belief: The Vision*, you're going to hit Decision Points where you choose a path. Whichever route you choose to go down in this level, stick with it. It's not a puzzle, and you're not going to be asked to do anything jokes, like run down the high street painted orange. If you want to get the most out of *Take Control,* you'll really need to throw yourself into each task. I'm not gonna know if you haven't really done the challenges in the book, but *you* will. And I do think that if you want to get anywhere, you'll need to throw yourself into it. Don't be scared to fail. It doesn't matter what anyone else thinks (and I'll tell you why, later). Be fearless, be focused.

Now it's time to choose a page and decide what happens next. What do you want to do?

Widen your horizons   **p 20**

Get on with it: you're ready, already   **p 22**

**Gain self-belief and increase
your confidence**   **p 24**

STAGE 1: WIDEN YOUR HORIZONS

It's all about you

Let's do this thing! By choosing this route I already feel like I know a little bit about the kind of person you are, and what you might be willing to do to put your idea into practice. Hopefully you're the kind of person who isn't too worried about what other people are up to, because you're focused on what *you* want to do. That's good.

When I was a kid, I didn't care too much if people thought I was foolish. But I *did care* about what I was gonna do when I got older. I used to see homeless people on the street and think, 'I don't wanna end up like that.' It was always in the back of my mind, even when I was young. At first I thought I wanted to be an actor, because that was the culture I was surrounded by – TV, the Internet and magazines were all about singers, actors, footballers, all living a glam lifestyle.

I used to watch TV and want to be in S Club 7. In primary school we literally used to play S Club 7 as a game, and I used to be Bradley, and someone else was Jo, and someone was Rachel. We used the cones from outside the school gates and set them up as if they were a stage, pretending to have mikes and putting on a 'live performance' at lunchtime or after school. I don't think that's cheesy, because it was primary school. It was when S Club 7 were massive and it looked to me like their life was pretty good :)

But it's not always a good idea to focus too much on wanting to be famous, because you need to start building your own vision, and coming up with your own ideas, rather than waiting for someone to discover you. That almost never happens and although there's always a little luck and timing involved when people make it, the truth is, it's mostly about hard work. So you have a choice. You can wait for things to happen to you, or you can make them happen for yourself.

So the first thing I think we should do – and I think you can take it – is to stop thinking about what everyone else thinks, and start thinking like you did back when you were a kid. Those times when you were having so much fun you forgot to be embarrassed or worry about who was watching. With that in mind, you're going to make another decision...

DECISION POINT

Now it's time to choose what happens next – what is it going to be?

Enter the bubble   **p 28**
Switch up the scenery   **p 31**

STAGE 1: GET ON WITH IT: YOU'RE READY, ALREADY

I was lucky to be quite popular at school, and I had lots of friends, so I identify with other confident people. I like to employ them at SB.TV, because it's fun to work with people who are cool with themselves, and who don't mind me having loud music on or dancing in the office. Maybe you're someone like that, and you've already worked out what you want, and how you're gonna get there. I'm wondering if that's why you chose this path.

But I think it's important to make sure that you don't close yourself off from other paths when you're just starting out, even if you have a strong idea about who you are and don't think you're going to change. When you're young – especially if you're living at home – you have more freedom than you're ever likely to have again. And so it's crazy not to use that time to experiment and try out loads of new things, whether it's doing some work experience at a local company or volunteering with a charity.

I've done things in the last couple of years I never thought I would do when I was fifteen, but I do remember having to negotiate with my mum at that age. When I started SB.TV she was always on at me to make sure I didn't get kicked out of college. All I really wanted to be doing was making videos, but we made a deal that she would let me out at night to film MCs and artists, if I agreed to finish my college course. That felt like an adult thing to do, making that compromise.

So maybe it's too early to have a fixed idea about who you are, maybe you're not the finished article – yet. Even if you genuinely do think you have all the skills you need to start your own venture, it might be worth checking. So before I send you back to the start, I'm gonna ask you do one thing.

Get some feedback

You might not feel comfortable doing this, but trust me, it'll be worth it.

1. Ask someone (a tutor, parent or manager – but maybe not one of your mates, you don't want to fall out!) to write a list of the five skills they think you're best at. But they're not allowed to talk about it in school, college or work terms. So no 'Jamal is good at English', 'Jamal is good at sport' or 'Jamal is good at accounts' – you want them to assess you as a person, so you can see what skills you bring to the table if you want to make an idea or business happen.
2. While they're doing it, you need to make your own list, of the top five things you're good at.
3. Then compare the two: have a think about whether their list matches yours. Next do the same, but with areas that you aren't so good at.

Be honest with yourself, and make sure you're able to figure out what your weaknesses are, because a great boss is someone who knows how to hire the people who are good at the things they're not so hot at.

Now you know areas you need to work on, I'm gonna send you back to choose another path on **p 19**.

STAGE 1: GAIN SELF-BELIEF AND INCREASE YOUR CONFIDENCE

Confidence and arrogance are two different things, I think. You can be confident and still be a nervous person. I think I'm quite nervous sometimes; I can be quiet in some situations when I'm trying to work out who everyone is or what's going on. But I do know what I'm good at and I don't think that's arrogant. If you don't know what you're good at you're never gonna be able to communicate that to other people or get them excited about what you're doing.

When I've done a good video, I will know when it's sick, and when we've got some good stuff down. I'll clap myself when that happens. And that's important too, because you need to know when you've done a good job so that you know that this piece of work – whatever it is, a video, a piece of clothing, a design – is finished. Then you can know that you're ready to put it out there in the world. You need to have an internal set of standards.

Although I've always been a confident kind of person, I still started out small, and got a lot more confident as I went along. I also made a few mistakes, but I'm not as worried about making mistakes as a lot of people are, or maybe I'm more optimistic about the fact that if I do something, I'm going to do a good job. That's how I want you to think, too. It's important that you're bold and brave about whatever you're doing, and have loads of self-belief.

Fake it till you make it

The first trick is give yourself permission to be someone else. I'm not saying there's anything wrong with you! But I do know plenty of people who 'faked it till they made it.' And by that I just mean pretending you're a confident person until you naturally become one. This can really work. So like, if you feel weird about being in a new environment or in front of a load of new people, try pretending you're a journalist who's been sent to cover an event. Keep your head up high, and remember that shyer people are often really good at noticing details, because they're really aware of what everyone is doing. If you're an expert in people, you could end up being great at marketing because this needs someone who understands all different kinds of people and knows exactly how to appeal to them. That could be you.

Here are some things to try:

1. If you have a job, go up to the executive floor of wherever you work, and talk to someone up there. Even if it's just to ask them the time or where the photocopier is. Say 'hi' and get used to being around powerful people and seeing how they act. Don't put powerful people on a pedestal, they're just people like you. The only difference is that they've been in the game longer.

2. Make a point of making more eye contact with strangers. Not staring people down until they think you're crazy – just being more open to other people. It doesn't matter if you're just in a shop being served by someone, or at the supermarket. Smile more, make more eye contact, dare yourself to start a conversation. You've got nothing to lose, and it's good practice for when you're talking to someone powerful who could help you achieve your idea.

3. If you're not already on Twitter, set up an account.
    Some people don't use Twitter because they think it's
    stupid, but it's only stupid if you post stupid stuff. Start
    posting links to things you're interested in — whether it's
    music, art, design, fashion, comedy, whatever. Get used
    to expressing your opinions in public until it feels
    normal. Follow people who are doing stuff you're into.
    Talk to them and a few other random people and see
    what happens. This is about networking and finding
    people who think like you. And don't be put off if you
    don't get replies, like all types of networking, it takes
    time to build up connections.

4. Sing in public. Yes, that's what I said!! Don't over-think
    it, just do it as you're walking along the street, when
    your favourite song comes on. And each time you try
    it, sing a bit louder. If you want to see any idea
    through, you have to become focused and
    unselfconscious — because otherwise you spend far
    too much time worrying about what everyone else is
    thinking. When you sing in public, you start to realise
    that if someone else doesn't like what you're doing, it's
    their problem.

If you've managed to do a couple of those things, you should
be proud — it's not easy putting yourself out there and if it's
not something you feel comfortable doing, it's even harder.
Let me know how you got on, even if it didn't go well. Tweet me
@selfbelievers and tell me what happened.

DECISION POINT

OK, now it's time to have a think about where you are. Maybe you're one of those people who has a really loud critical voice in their head which is always trying to give reasons why you shouldn't do something – 'it'll be too hard', 'everyone will laugh', 'I don't know how.' If you want to achieve anything you have to turn this voice off. Think of it like an annoying little devil on your shoulder. Do we need to crush him? Or maybe you feel like you're ready to do some more challenges, open yourself up to opportunities a bit more.

So what's it going to be?

Crush your shoulder devil   **p 37**

Say yes to everything   **p 34**

STAGE 2: **ENTER THE BUBBLE**

One thing I've learned from doing SB.TV is to try not to look at other people and what they're doing too much. You need to chase your dream, not the competition. I call this 'being in The Bubble.' I do this because if I look at other people it will cloud my mind, and maybe I'll start to think I'm not doing my job well enough. So for me and SB.TV I have to avoid looking at BBC or MTV too much, in case I start to think, 'Oh, maybe my intros aren't as good as theirs' or 'Their logos are better than ours.' I'm not saying it's not good to look at what other people are doing every now and then, but don't fixate on it. When I used to fixate, it would get me down, but I wouldn't be looking at my competitors objectively or remembering how many people they had working for them. At that stage, it was just me by myself – and when you're on your own, that kind of thinking can mess you up.

When I watched TV I would see something good and wonder why I couldn't do it, forgetting that what I was watching was made by like, a million-pound company. I was doing SB.TV from my bedroom. I would think, 'Why is the wind blowing on my mic in my videos, aaaaaaagh?' or I'd be jealous because they were getting to interview all these celebrities that I wanted to talk to. But that kind of thinking is dumb, because I wasn't taking into account that they had a lot more people working for them – and a lot more money.

Switch off, zone in

The other thing about 'The Bubble' is that the media and the Internet can be really distracting. Only you know how much time you spend messing about on stuff like Facebook, but it's good to analyse if that time is helping you get to where you want to be. And I feel like a lot of the mainstream media is bull. It just fills your head with a load of crap to get you scared of the world. I've gone through phases where I won't listen to the radio, read the papers or watch TV, and I get the clearest state of mind I've ever had, because I'm not letting all this rubbish get in my head.

I was in a cab recently and the cabbie was listening to some talk show. They were talking about the Queen having something wrong with her belly, and like Prince William *was gonna run the country* and it was *all gonna go downhill* and the Queen's gonna *DIE*. I was like, 'What? Turn this off!' I don't need that kind of thing on my Monday morning. That sort of stuff, I try not to let it get to me, and I blank it out.

So this week I want you to enter The Bubble:

- Stop looking at Facebook, Twitter, TV, the radio, magazines, video games, just block it all out – that's The Bubble.
- While you're in The Bubble, I want you to make a list – in your head, or on your phone, or on paper – of the things you want to do.
- Dream BIG: think about where you want to be; what kind of job you want to do. Work out if you see yourself earning your own money, or getting a promotion at work, or starting a website. It doesn't matter what your idea is, just think about the things you enjoy doing or who you admire the most, and visualise what you want your future to look like.

The only thing you're not allowed to do while you're brainstorming is to start thinking about how, what or why. Don't put any barriers in front of your ideas or think of reasons why it can't happen to you. Sometimes you need to be in The Bubble, to just be in your own thing :)

DECISION POINT

Now it's time to make a choice so you can move to the
next stage, because it's time to start working on your
idea from a practical perspective. Do you want to:

Buy some stuff for your idea   p 40
Pitch your idea to a stranger   p 42

STAGE 2: SWITCH UP THE SCENERY

Be where you want to be

When I started to get some serious hits on SB.TV, I needed to work on it every day. Every day after school, every day after work. I was always editing videos. My work ethic was definitely part of what got me where I am now. I would travel in the snow or make long bus journeys, if it meant filming somebody good. I didn't care where the artists I wanted to film were, or how long it took to get there. Regardless how my videos turned out in the beginning, I was always visible online, without fail. And people started to notice because they were always like, 'Jamal, you're always here, man!' I made *sure* I was always there.

So my point is that wherever you wanna be, wherever you wanna work, or whatever scene you want to be part of, you have to *be there*. Be there. You need to be where things are happening. If you want to work for the BBC, be there. If you want to design clothes for Topshop, be there.

Like I said, I took the long way round from work, just to walk past the BBC. Because I knew that, not every day, but some days, I would see someone I could maybe talk to or film. It's the maddest thing, and people don't realise, but it's that simple. If I wanted to work in Jamie Oliver's restaurant, I would eat in there all the time. I would get friendly with the people who work there.

You need to be around like-minded people because it helps you get to know the environment you want to work in or the community you want to be part of. You also need to be a friendly person. And you've *got* to be visible. Standing out is really important, regardless of what you want to do.

But switching up the scenery is also about seeing beyond your own world, outside your own patch. I know a lot of kids who spend all their time on their estate or with the same mates, and they all go to the same places, week in, week out. I'm not sure that's always a good thing. You need to get out and see the world before you can really find your right place in it. Like, you might not ever have been to an art gallery, because you've already decided you're not the kind of person who goes to one. Some people have never been out raving. Why not? Why would you not want to try new things? It makes no sense.

Change it up

So for the next week, I want you to switch up your scenery. This is taking the idea in the first challenge and going a bit further with it. Give some of the following a go:

- Start going out to places you don't normally go: walk down streets you've never been down before; get a feel for the vibe of a few new places.
- Listen to what people are talking about.
- Look at what other people are wearing.
- Read a different blog or newspaper to the one you normally do.
- Start talking to people you don't know – not necessarily random people, not the crazies on the bus! I want you to talk to the kind of people whose numbers you want in your phone; the kind of people who might be able help you do your thing.
- Ask a friend for a playlist if he's into some mad noise you don't know anything about.
- Get a library card.

- Go to your local youth club.
- Post something on a forum thread.
- Read a new magazine or try to get a letter printed in a paper.

Do as many things that 'aren't like you' as you possibly can. Remember that whether you want to set up a business or start a campaign group in your community, you're going to need to inspire people from all walks of life. So if you don't normally go to art galleries, go to one, sit in the cafe and listen to the people who hang out there.

You need to understand people from all walks of life and how to talk to them and get to them on their level. You need to know where they hang out, online and in real life, if you want to market your ideas at them. Because one day you'll have to convince people who aren't your mates. And you'll need to get used to meeting new people. Because one day you might have to persuade a suit to invest money in your ideas, or find someone to work for you, or persuade someone to become your mentor.

At the end of the week, you should have a fresh outlook both on who you are and who you share the planet with. Maybe you've seen some new stuff you wanna share with me on Twitter? Tweet me @selfbelievers.

DECISION POINT

Now it's time to make a choice. Do you want to:

Surprise yourself	**p 45**
Take a time out – you don't feel ready	**p 49**

STAGE 2: **SAY YES TO EVERYTHING**

Everything is an opportunity

When I started SB.TV I never turned down any opportunity, even if I knew I was going to have a hard time making it happen. If someone wanted me to film them, I would agree to do it, even if I had no idea how to get there or no money for the bus. So that's what I want you to do for a week: you have to say 'yes' to every opportunity that comes your way.

- If someone invites you out and you don't think it's your scene, go anyway.
- If your tutor or a work colleague talks about an event that's happening or a competition/prize you could enter, go to that event and enter that competition.
- If someone wants to collaborate with you on some art or music, just do it, see what happens.
- The only rule is that you're not allowed to overthink it. This task is all about speed.

Saying 'yes' is a good way to push yourself and put yourself to the test. And you should do more of that pushing early on in your career, because later on down the line it's difficult to get out of things as you'll have many more commitments. When you're younger, you have to do mad things that at first seem like they're impossible, just to raise your game. Everyone's capable of doing superhuman stuff, and I think you'll surprise yourself. When you say 'yes' to something, you're making a commitment to another person. And that pressure – that they need you to follow-up on your promise of 'yes' – is a good kind of pressure.

Sometimes I'd say 'yes' to things even though I *knew* I couldn't do it. So Tinchy Stryder would be like, 'I'll see you at the show in Sheffield tomorrow!' and I'd be like, 'Yeah, bro!' – even though inside I was like, 'Er, *no*, how am I gonna get there?' I managed to persuade my friend Billy to drive me to Sheffield on the morning of that show, I was like, 'Pleeeeeeeease, drive me.' But that's the point; you find a way. Even if every project is going to clash, even if you don't have time to eat or sleep. *Especially* when you don't know how you're going to make it work.

Of course there'll be times where this trips you up and you say 'yes' to something but end up having to pull out because even though you've moved heaven and earth, you can't make it happen – even if you had a million pounds. That's only happened once or twice in my whole career. And when that happened, obviously I emailed the people, said I was sorry and made it up to them another day, so it was cool. But saying 'yes' to everything at the beginning is vital.

When to say 'no'

Later on, once you've started your business or put your idea into practice, and when you've said 'yes' to so many things, you have the chance to say 'no'. Now I'm established, I'm focused on what I want to do, and I don't have to be at everyone's beck and call or say 'yes' to everything just to get my name out there. Now I'm at the stage where I have a choice. But that only happened at the beginning of 2013. I'm saying that if you say 'yes' for long enough, the work and the business will start to come to you, and you won't have to spend so much time chasing it.

When you've done the task in this stage, it's time to go for a walk or go somewhere quiet and start to have a proper think. I want you to make a list – in your head, or on your phone, or on paper – of the things you want to do. Dream BIG. Think about where you want to be; what kind of job you want to do. Work out if you see yourself earning your own money, or getting a promotion at work, or starting a website. It doesn't matter what your idea is, just think about the things you enjoy doing or admire the most, and visualise what you want your future to look like.

The only thing you're not allowed to do while you're brainstorming is to start thinking about how, what or why. Don't put any barriers in front of your ideas or think of reasons why it can't happen to you.

DECISION POINT

Now it's time to make a choice so you can move to the next stage, because it's time to start working on your idea from a practical perspective. Do you want to:

Buy some stuff for your idea   **p 40**

Pitch your idea to a stranger   **p 42**

STAGE 2: CRUSH YOUR SHOULDER DEVIL

In early 2013 I had to do a big press launch for the Manchester International Festival, because I'd been asked to curate three nights of music for it. But I was the only inner-city kid there and Kenneth Branagh was sitting next to me, talking to me about doing *Macbeth*. I was like, 'Yeah, I'm doing some grime shows...' It was quite jokes. I was proud to be one of the twenty commissioners, because stuff like that puts me on another level. And I've come from *this*.

To come from where I have, and be curating shows at this huge art festival, is just crazy. What I'm saying is that sometimes I get nervous too and I wonder what I'm doing in certain places. I can't believe where I've come from and how I got here. The main reason I think I've been able to do it is because I've always had a lot of self-belief.

Think what could happen, not what won't

If you're more self-critical, it can hold you back. Instead of getting excited about what you're doing, you'll be looking for reasons why your plans or ideas might fail. When I first started SB.TV, the main problem was access – I didn't know any celebrities, so I couldn't get interview time with anyone. I had to think about it from another perspective, which was to hang around outside hotels where footballers might be staying or if I knew there was a film premiere in town, I would see if I could find out where the actors were staying. I used to wait outside places.

One day I heard that Jason Statham was in Wardour Street, and I went down there with my camera and waited around for like an hour, two hours, to see if I could see him. Just so I could get on the chat with him. But he didn't come down.

Whenever anything like that happens I always think, 'One day, that person will know about me.' And that makes me feel better and helps me keep going. That kind of thing removes all negative talk. So now if I don't get an acoustic session with someone or I don't get to film them, I always think 'There'll be another time.'

However deluded it is, regardless if I'm interviewing 50 Cent and it gets cut short, I'll always be thinking, 'One day...' You have to think positive, and that's why I never think that something won't happen. I've proved it – because I've gone to 10 Downing Street and I've interviewed David Cameron and Richard Branson and John Legend. Those things *shouldn't* have been possible, but they did happen to me, and I think that's partly because I stayed positive and had faith that it would all turn out good.

Shake it off

If you're always thinking of reasons why you *can't* do something, or find it hard to quiet down that voice in your head that tells you you're *not* good at things, you have to deal with that. If I'm trying to work out problems, I go for a walk, I have some time alone or I go to the gym. It's so refreshing, and working out means all the stresses go – you feel amazing, it clears everything out of your brain. Try that this week – get some exercise in whatever way you like – whether it's a ten-minute dance break, walking the dog or joining a gym. As soon as you feel stressed, run!

There's loads of other tricks you can do to shake off negative patterns of thinking. For the next few days, why not try these things:

1. If you find that perfectionism stops you from trying new things, give yourself permission to be bad at them. When I started SB.TV my editing skills were jokes, but I got better. If I'd let being bad at editing stop me from making videos, there'd be no SB.TV.

2. Visualise your critical voice as an evil demon, holding you back. Then ask yourself why you're paying attention to someone who's not on your side? Just think about stamping on that demon. Crush it. Feel better?

3. Make a point of seeking out people who are positive and who support your vision. If your friends aren't into your thing, go online and join a forum of like-minded people.

DECISION POINT

Now it's time to make a choice. Do you want to:

Surprise yourself   **p 45**

Take a time out – you don't feel ready   **p 49**

STAGE 3: BUY SOME STUFF FOR YOUR IDEA

So one of the things that can stop people from pursuing their vision is when they think they need to have all the latest gear before they start. You have to try hard not to do this. So if you want to, I don't know, start your own blog – you might think, 'Right, I've got to buy myself all the latest software. And until I can get that I can't do anything.' This is upside down, though. Whatever field you're working in, you need to work with what you have, in baby steps, until you can afford to put more money into your idea.

When I started making videos for SB.TV I only had a £25 NEC flip-phone, one of the first phones that had a camera on it. Then it progressed and it was me, my PC and a handheld Panasonic camera I'd got as a present. And it was just that. That's what I had and all I could afford, so that's what I used to film people on my estate with. I had to edit footage with software like Windows Movie Maker or Cool Edit Pro. And I used to rinse all the effects on my videos, putting in so many screen transitions that the software literally wouldn't let me put any more in. So the videos just used to look cheap and tacky – I used the 'star' and the 'triangle' transitions, the red filter, loads of screen flashes. I chucked so much at each video, it made people dizzy, and they were jokes.

Work with what you've got

But everyone goes through a cheesy phase with whatever they're making or doing, because they're starting out. Although it was kind of like the video equivalent of using Comic Sans to design a shop sign, I can recognise now that I was just young and I didn't know any better. It's cool. The main thing I want you to realise is that I didn't let crap equipment stop me from filming. I just thought, 'This is all I have to work with, I just have to make the best of it.' And you have to go through those early stages, trying stuff out and seeing what works, if you want get good at anything.

When you start out you've gotta work with what you have – don't start making crazy shopping lists of stuff you need before you can get on with it. You need to start NOW and work towards buying yourself better stuff. Even if that means working on computers in your college or library because you don't have the Internet at home, or asking to borrow stuff off other people in return for doing them a favour. To succeed, you have to get yourself in a mindset where obstacles don't exist – whether they're barriers to do with money, or where you live, or what kind of person you think you are. In fact, you pretty much need to forget about stuff that might get in your way. The best way to do this is to let go of your inhibitions, go back to the Decision Point on **p 30** (if you came from Enter the Bubble) or **p 36** (if you came from Say Yes to Everything) and pitch your idea to a stranger this time.

STAGE 3: PITCH YOUR IDEA TO A STRANGER

The first time I had to explain SB.TV to someone I didn't know, I wasn't as slick as I would've liked. But pitching your vision to people is really important, because you've got to be able to 'sell' your ideas to people, especially if you want to find a good team to work with. If you can't explain your vision to them, how can you know if they 'get it' too?

When I started, some of the things I talked about in my emails to people – promoters, labels, artists, PRs – were mad. I didn't really know how things worked or how to approach people in the right way. But even if my approach wasn't the best, I think they could tell how enthusiastic I was and that I wasn't going to go away. As long as you're polite and keen, people will tend to think you're persistent, rather than annoying.

Pitch to people in a way they'll 'get'

When I wanted to get in with labels like Universal and Sony, I did loads of emailing, asking to do videos with their artists, asking people for contacts. I'd already got to know some people from those labels so I'd start hassling them, telling them what videos I'd already done and explaining what SB.TV was about, how many views and subscribers we were getting. But at that time, some people thought SB.TV was just about grimey, urban artists, so I needed to *change the conversation*. I needed major pop record labels to understand that the SB.TV audience – and all the subscribers – were open to stuff from a pop demographic, so they could see that being on SB.TV would benefit their pop artists too. I sent a lot of emails, every week; I *was* literally going in every week, checking in on them. There was a lot of that.

What you have to remember is that if you're trying to pitch an idea to someone – especially someone powerful– you have to keep it simple. If you're worried about the reaction your email might get, you'll probably over-explain things, because you're worried about how to talk to that person.

So once you've identified someone whose feedback you want, do some research – follow them on Twitter, look up their profile on LinkedIn, see what you can find out about who they are. Use whatever tricks you can to get their email address – again, search on Twitter, LinkedIn, About.Me, Facebook and every social media site you can think of – until you find some contact information. If you have to call their office, do it, don't be scared. It's good to be keen.

Practice makes perfect

The best way to practise pitching is to do it aloud, to someone else. See if you can explain your idea in one sentence, using words of one syllable, to a friend or one of your parents. Keep practising until you have it down. Then, when you email your idea, here's some good things to include in your email:

1. A compliment about that person in the first paragraph. Say you think their clothes are sick if you want, but it might be better to say you admire something they do in their job and that's why you're approaching them.
2. Put your idea forward in one sentence. So maybe, 'Basically, I wanted to get your feedback on an idea I've had. My idea is to_____.'
3. See if you can explain your idea as a way to solve a problem. So, I did SB.TV because I knew loads of grime MCs who weren't getting enough attention; I started a

YouTube channel to get them that attention. What problem are you solving?

4. Try to explain what's unique or different about your idea. Do you know more about this subject than other people? Or are you going to approach it in a new way?

5. See if you can work out why you're the best person to solve this problem. I was heavily immersed in the grime scene and knew a lot about it when I started filming MCs. That's why I was in a good place to start promoting urban UK music.

6. Paint a picture of what will happen if your idea doesn't come about. Are you starting a community group to campaign on issues that affect young people? What will happen if you don't start your group? Demonstrate there's a need for your community group/label/business.

Remember that if you've done something that you're proud of, you should shout about it. So if you've had a good idea or come up with a solution to a problem, don't get into the trap of thinking that it's arrogant to talk about that idea. If you do something and you feel proud, you should tell people. It just shows that you're on your job.

DECISION POINT

We're pretty much at the end of Level 1 now!! Are you buzzing? Are you feeling more confident about your ideas? Or maybe things didn't go quite how you wanted them to? Be honest with yourself. So, how'd it go?

Boom! Success	**p 51**
OK, but I might need to try again	**p 53**
Oh my days it was bad	**p 55**

STAGE 3: **SURPRISE YOURSELF**

Stuff doesn't happen unless you make it happen

So far, I've tried to make you think about doing new things or increasing your self-belief. Now I want you to come up with some ideas about what you actually want *to do*. You probably know some people who've always known what they wanted to be – and in some ways it's easier for people like that.

If you're really good at biology and you get this kind of calling that you want to be a doctor, then your path is kind of mapped out, early. But if you're into loads of different things, it can be harder. Some people don't get that wake-up call until much later in life. They suddenly realise they don't want to be a teacher or office worker or whatever, and then in their thirties they decide to set up their own business and like, run a farm and make cheese.

I think it's better to challenge yourself when you're young and try to make a decision. To make that choice, it can be better to focus less on what you're best at, and instead pursue what you enjoy the most. For me, it was music. If you pursue something you love, you'll have the energy and drive to get better at it and there's far less chance of you being bored along the way.

I remember watching voice-over videos when YouTube first started and thinking, 'I could do one of those.' I was late on it because there were already loads of them. But I was also genuinely fascinated by why these foxes were in my garden and why they were making so much noise and waking me up at night. So I did a video with a voice-over like Steve Irwin, with all the 'Crikeys!' and 'Oh my God, it's coming!' things he did. And I think people found the commentary funny, because I filmed it in the dark and you couldn't really see what was happening. So it ended up getting loads of hits.

Then I realised that I couldn't just wait for more foxes making crazy noises to be in my garden every night, but I needed to do something else to keep up the momentum. So I just did other random stuff like filming my mum making macaroni cheese (it is really nice macaroni cheese, but I don't know why I thought other people would wanna watch it!) All the time I was learning about what worked, and didn't work, on YouTube. A load of my mates were MCs, so I decided to use the skills I'd got to film them.

So although it looks like I just 'decided' at fifteen what I wanted to do, there was a journey and it began with me being proactive. Stuff can't happen to you, unless you make stuff happen. Now it's time for you to start.

What makes you hyped?

OK, now I want you to write a list of the top five times in your life when you had the most fun. What were you doing? It doesn't matter if it was a school, college or a sport thing. Look at those five things and work out:

a) If you can make a career out of them.

b) Which ones you'd be able to do every day for the longest, and not get bored by.

It doesn't matter if you can only imagine a few years into the future, because having to decide WHAT YOU WANT TO DO FOR THE REST OF YOUR LIFE is kind of stupid. We're talking about now and taking action now.

When you've got your list of potential careers (however mad they might be), you need to contact someone who does it for a job. Use whatever tools you can to get their email address – search on Twitter, About.Me, Facebook or wherever – until you get a contact address.

All I want you to do is write a three-line email to them, asking if they would be up for giving you advice. Either use my example below or write your own. Don't be afraid to be cheeky and play on the fact that you're young to get advice. Tell 'em Jamal sent you. Let's get people talking about *Self Belief: The Vision* and start some networks!

Try something along the lines of:

Hi

My name is _____ and I'm ____ years old. I'm reading Jamal Edwards' book *Self Belief: The Vision*, and I've decided I want to work in music/TV/fashion/food (delete as appropriate). I think you're amazing/ inspirational/sick.

Would you be willing to give me five minutes of your time so I can ask how you got into your line of work? I'd really appreciate it.

Kind regards

Then hit send!

DECISION POINT

What happened when you sent your email? We're hitting the end of Level 1, so it's time to look at how it went for you. So how'd you get on?

Boom! Success   **p 51**

OK, but I might need to try again   **p 53**

Oh my days it was bad   **p 55**

STAGE 3: TAKE A TIME OUT – YOU DON'T FEEL READY

I had a big wake-up call when I was in college and my form tutor said, 'Look, the headmaster wants to kick you out, but I'm trying to save you, you need to sort it out.' I was bunking lessons and not handing in work because of SB.TV – it was low level, but I just had bad concentration. I was doing videos and I thought most of the lessons weren't engaging enough for me; I felt like I already knew what they were trying to teach me because I was already making videos.

But I had two teachers who were the most meaningful to me, called Gareth and Ashleyne, and they kept me occupied. I had a camera lesson and a planning lesson, coming up with plans and then executing them. We were learning how to come up with a strategy for how we would film a particular product and then we'd have to make the videos. They were the lessons that I got the best marks in.

I think it's normal to get to a point where you don't want to be pushed. I was there myself, when I was in college. But ultimately I ended up making a deal with my mum so she would let me go out and make videos for SB.TV, if I finished my college course. So I got my head down and got my National Diploma in Media (Moving Image). And obviously that came in handy, because I learned stuff I've been able to use at SB.TV. I'm so glad I finished that course, because it did open doors.

The main thing to remember is that whether you have a good support network around you or not, it's only you who can make stuff happen for yourself. You have to look inside yourself and work out why you don't want to get on with the rest of your life, whether it's out of fear or a lack of self-belief, or because you don't know how to make the first step. Take time out now to think about that, get some exercise, listen to some music and be honest with yourself. I promise you that if you push yourself, you can achieve anything. When you are ready, go back to the Decision Point on **p 33** (if you came from Switch Up the Scenery) or **p 39** (if you came from Crush Your Shoulder Devil).

END OF LEVEL 1: **BOOM! SUCCESS**

We're reaching the end of *Take Control* now, and you've either pitched an idea to someone or written to someone to ask for advice. If you got a positive reply, that is sick. Seriously, that is sick. People get hundreds of emails, texts, tweets and messages every day, so just getting a reply is really cool. If they were positive about your idea too, that is amazing, so get in touch and tell me what happened – tweet me @selfbelievers, I wanna hear your stories.

The first thing you need to do is reply to thank whoever's given you useful comments. I always do this when someone has taken the time to give me considered feedback – even if it isn't positive. So write back straight away. At the very least, you should try to support them in what they're doing, like by RTing them on Twitter or offering to support their work in some way.

The second thing you need to do is put this person into your address book. I always keep in touch with people – especially people who were supportive from day one, from way back. That way I can update them whenever something good happens. If someone has bothered to write to you then they've kind of invested in your story already, and the 'payback' for them will be to hear from you when you manage to implement their advice or find success. When I got the Google advert or was on the front cover of *Wired* magazine, I made a point of telling those people who first helped me and gave me work experience placements. I also always send them a nice message at Christmas.

You also never know if this person could be useful to you in future – they may end up being your mentor or working with you. So see if this email could be the beginning of a dialogue, rather than a full stop.

And that's the end of this level. Why don't you head back to the start and try some different paths this time? That way you'll get to do more tasks and pick up some more tips. If you want to give this level another go, go to **p 7**. If not, see you soon on **p 57** for Level 2!

END OF LEVEL 1: OK, BUT I MIGHT NEED TO TRY AGAIN

First off, well done – you've made it to the end of Level 1. That means you've either pitched an idea to someone or written to someone to ask for advice. That takes guts, especially if you've not got massive confidence, so you've gotta be proud of that.

I'm guessing if you're feeling a bit mixed about how you did it's because you got some negative comments. It can really sting, I get it. But this is part of the journey. If everyone liked your idea straight off, it would never get the chance to become something miles better. You'd get lazy and think you'd got it all down.

So take another look at the comments that made you really mad. (I don't mean people being stupid and saying stuff for the sake of it.) Things where people have said something criticising your idea, and it got to you. Did it annoy you because they might be a bit right? Not totally, but there's maybe something in what they've said that you could take on board?

Whatever, I want you to make a point of thanking the people who gave you negative feedback – thank the people who were nice too – but I want you to do this so you're learning how to accept the not-so-good stuff along with the compliments.

If you didn't get as many replies as you'd hoped to get, try sending a follow-up email a week or two later. You're not spamming them if it's just one or two, so give it a go. You don't lose anything. Just don't get mad at them for not replying or whine in your email. Keep it light, confident and GO FOR IT!

And that's the end of Level 1. It sounds like you could go back and have a go at some other options on this level, to get that self-belief back where it needs to be. The more you practise these things now, the more wicked your idea's gonna get later on, so take the time. Go to **p 7** to take you back, or if you think you know where your head's at and want to move on, I'll see you on **p 57** at Level 2...

END OF LEVEL 1: OH MY DAYS IT WAS BAD

OK, you're being a bit down on yourself, so let's have a look at why.

1. You didn't get a reply

OK, it's worth spending a little time trying to work out why. Get someone else (a parent or tutor maybe) to look over your email. Was it professional enough? Did you spell their name right? Little things like this are important, because if you don't look like you took time over your email, they won't feel like helping you. But don't spend too long thinking about this because it'll mess you up. Move on, write another email to someone else. Keep going. They might just have been really busy – ultimately you'll probably never know why they didn't reply, so it's pointless spending ages thinking about it. Try sending a second email and see what happens.

2. They weren't nice

If they were really critical, then see it as a GOOD thing. Maybe they spotted something wrong with your idea which will save you loads of time and work down the line. If so, they might have done you a favour. If you don't agree with their feedback then get a second opinion.

The main thing is to learn from this – each email you send out is JUST AN EMAIL. Right now just writing it and sending it out is the thing you need to focus on. You're reaching out and that's good.

It sounds like you need to big yourself up a bit so let's give this level another go. Try some different options, and look at the good stuff that comes out of each bit. There WILL be good stuff, you're just not seeing it.

You've got loads of time to fix up, it's OK. Go to **p7** to go back to the start of Level 1.

Or maybe after thinking about it, and looking at why you felt it was bad, you're feeling a bit better and want to step up to Level 2. In which case go to the page opposite, I'll see you there!

THE
KNOWLEDGE

Level 2

FOREWORD

From the moment I met Jamal, it was evident that he has faith. He has faith in ideas, in people and, most importantly, faith that all things are possible. This combination of complete certainty and a formidable work ethic has resulted in a truly inspiring story of young entrepreneurship.

I've had the opportunity to work closely with Jamal, and have not only watched, but also learnt an enormous amount as SB.TV has grown from humble beginnings to the phenomenon it is now. And this is only the beginning. Jamal continues to explore and move into other business areas with the same intense passion, determination and drive that he applied when first starting out.

In this book he will share the experiences that have shaped his career and will help you prepare as you take your first steps in the world of business.

There may be no guarantee of success, but by reading what he has to say your chances will, unquestionably, be greatly improved.

Emeli Sandé, 2013

THE KNOWLEDGE

INTRO

This level is about getting the essential information for you to succeed. It's about that point in your life when you decide to pursue an idea, but need to get all your facts together before you can move forward. When I started SB.TV I was on a Media and Moving Image course at college, so I was learning all the time about how to plan videos and then edit them so they'd be the kind of thing that other young people would want to watch. I wanted this book to be about that time, to help guide you through the different ways you can arm yourself with skills and come up with a concrete plan for how you turn your vision into a reality.

Level 2 is 'The Knowledge', where you'll start getting your ideas down and find out what you need to know about the area you want to get into, whether that's music, running a caf, or just getting an idea off the ground at college or work.

So, you with me? Let's do this.

MY STORY

How I learnt the ropes...

I didn't have media entrepreneurs in my family. A lot of them worked for Vauxhall, so it wasn't as if I had people around me who could teach me about running a business like SB.TV. But I read a lot, and I would go on the Internet until I could find out what I needed to know. I mean, my mum did buy me a load of the *Dummies Guide To...* books, but I never read them because they were so thick. She gave me one on accounts and some business books and I was like, 'Are you being serious?' But even though I didn't read them, I knew my mum was teaching me that if I didn't have the answer to something, someone else always would. And you should always remember that when you get stuck.

My dad was pretty smart too, he got good grades at school and he always had a good sense about money – he works as a mortgage adviser now and used to work as a stockbroker. The main thing is that they were always really supportive, they always believed in me and told me, 'You can do this, Jamal.' You need to surround yourself with people like that, if you don't have them in your family. Because they taught me that you should always try something, and if it doesn't work out, it doesn't matter, because you can try it again and do it another way, until you get there. They taught me that anything was possible, if you put your mind to it. So my journey was part instinct, and part research. A lot of people think that if they try something once and it fails, they should just forget it, but that's wrong. I remember going at it for long hours. Research is important: you can't go round thinking, 'It's not fair, nobody ever taught me that stuff!' You have to find out for yourself.

Taking risks

One time I was interviewing Nicki Minaj and her PR person said I couldn't get in the lift with her after the interview was finished. But I really wanted to get more footage from the point of view of Nicki coming out of the Dorchester hotel, with all the fans screaming, because there were bare paps and I knew it would look sick on film. So I just got into the lift with Nicki and carried on filming her.

I don't even think she knew if I was meant to be in the lift with her, so nobody said anything. In music and media, it's so strict: you get your set time with the artist and that is IT. But I really wanted this footage. I edited it as soon as I got back and we put it up on SB.TV and by the next day there were already over 100,000 views on it. Then I got a call from the record label saying, 'Nice video Jamal!' even though they told me the day before that I couldn't film it! Then they brought me on to do two more videos for her outside my interview, which is rare.

I'm not saying acting like this is always a good idea, because it could have gone really wrong and I could have messed up my whole career. I could really have pissed off her record label, which has loads of other artists that I wanted to work with. They could have pulled the whole interview. So it was a big risk. And it might not have worked. But it did :)

How I got work experience

When I was a teenager I really wanted to get a part-time job because I didn't have any money and I needed to get a decent computer and camera. I'd been trying for ages to get a job and I'd gone and asked absolutely everywhere.

One day I'd been taking my CV round all the shops, and I got home a bit downhearted. So my mum said she would take me round – and she basically frogmarched me into Topman and said, 'Give my son a job.' It was so embarrassing. They were saying, 'No, we don't have any jobs going,' but she wouldn't take no for an answer, she said, 'I don't care, he'll work for free, you *have* to take him on.' And they agreed, probably because they just wanted to get rid of her; they wanted us to leave.

At first I was only taken on as a work experience person, but it became a regular part-time job after I'd proved myself. And now I'm really grateful that she did that, and embarrassed me, because I needed that job. And if I hadn't had a part-time job when I started SB.TV, it would have been much, much harder.

THINGS TO THINK ABOUT

OK, for *Level 2: The Knowledge*, you're going to be finding out more about the area you want to get into, and that's going to take some guts as you'll have to speak to people you don't know, ask them questions and push yourself forward.

It's really important to take a few risks – and risk embarrassing yourself – when you have an idea that you want to see through. And trust me, once you've taken that leap once, you'll get over yourself and be much more confident at giving new things a go.

Whether you're planning to hit someone up for advice or do some research, or if you need access to a person or place, it can pay to be cheeky. You can always blame it on youthful foolishness later, because people kind of expect young people to do mad things, and I think you can use that belief to your advantage.

THE CHALLENGE

For the next week, I want cheekiness to be your thing. I want you to get out there and ambush people, see who you can get in front of – people who can help you get your idea off the ground or give you good advice. So some different situations might be...

- Getting yourself into a club because you want to meet the promoter
- Waiting outside the office of someone powerful because they have advice or information you need
- Ringing someone up and seeing if you can get a meeting with them
- Seeing if you can interview someone about their journey to the top

This week should be all about taking a slightly mischievous route to getting the info and skills you need. Here are some tips:

Keep it light and be polite

The point about being cheeky is that in order to get away with it, you have to be really happy, generous and polite. Happy, confident, breezy people are hard to get annoyed with, especially if you pay loads of compliments to the person you want something from. You'll probably already know that if you've ever had a row with your mum, they don't like it when you get all whiney or sneaky about stuff. So I'm not suggesting you lie or act nasty, just that you have a go at asking for stuff instead of being all reserved all the time. Push yourself forward. Ask for discounts in shops. Treat networking like you were asking someone out – smile, laugh, be positive.

Don't think too hard

You're also not allowed to over-think things this week. You've got my permission to do stuff without having some kind of breakdown about all the possibilities of *what could go wrong* or *what if I mess it up.* That kind of thinking is out of the question. Whatever your idea is – and especially if you're planning to get into a majorly competitive industry like fashion or music or TV – you'll be up against lots of other really ambitious people.

So you need to stand out as a fun, hard-working person, who makes stuff happen without getting all stressed and negative. I know they say 'look before you leap' but sometimes that's not true – and it's especially not true of entrepreneurs. Partly that's because they're less afraid of failure; they know that if one thing fails, another thing will come along. For every door that closes, another opens.

So go on, try it for a week and tweet me @selfbelievers to tell me what happened, and what or where being cheeky got you.

DECISION POINT

OK, so you've got yourself in the right frame of mind. Now it's time to make a choice as you move into Stage 1 of *The Knowledge*. Do you want to:

Come up with a master plan	**p 67**
Find people to work on your idea	**p 71**
Start researching your idea	**p 73**

STAGE 1: COME UP WITH A MASTER PLAN

Now you're done being cheeky, it's time to make a plan. This isn't really a traditional business plan, it's more a way of working out what you're going to do, and how you're going to do it. Keep it factual and specific, and use what you write down as a way of tracking your progress. If you wake up every day thinking, 'I need to get a recording contract,' you're always going to be stressing out, because that is such a big thing to do. But if you break it down, you can do a small task every day, tick it off and feel like you're moving forward.

Go into lockdown

The first thing you need to do is make sure you're not distracted. Make sure you're working somewhere where you won't be disturbed. Turn your phone off, unplug the internet if you need to – only you know what things you get distracted by. It's up to you to decide if Facebook/Twitter/PS3/Xbox are stopping you from achieving things, and whether you're OK with it if they are. Try giving your passwords to someone you trust and ask them to change them so you can't log into the sites you waste the most time on. Or use some site-blocking software or an add-on.

One thing that always helped me stay focused – especially when I started SB.TV – would be to make sure that I didn't stop whatever task I was working on until it was totally finished. I would always keep going until it was done, even if that meant I was up all night. If you're not very good at remembering to do things, put some reminders in your phone. Or put a Post-it on the wall. Basically, be honest with yourself, and use whatever method will work and that you have a chance of sticking to.

Be real with yourself

Now, the plan. All you need to do is answer the following questions. You can use this structure for tackling any problem really, and hopefully it'll focus your mind and make you think about the logistics of your idea – whether it's for a business, or if you just want to achieve something in your life. Below are ten questions and beneath them are what my answers would have been seven years ago, to help you think what your answers would be. Have a read and write down your responses:

1. What is your idea?

I want to start an online TV channel to promote UK urban music called SB.TV.

2. What makes you the right person to do this?

I've studied how to film and edit videos at college, I know loads of up-and-coming MCs/grime artists, and I'm all over social media.

3. How will you make your idea work?

I'll travel to the artists, film them using my camera, edit them on my computer, upload them to YouTube and then promote them using social media. I will have a very quick turnaround, editing the videos the same day I film them.

4. How much will you charge? (if it's relevant)

I won't charge if they can't afford it, but if I'm working for an established or major label artist, I'll charge a production fee. I will also get income from advertising on my videos.

5. Who is your idea targeted at and how will you reach them?

This TV channel is aimed at people like me, mainly between the ages of 14–25, and I will target them through the social media channels they already use, like MySpace and Bebo.

6. Does anyone else already do this? (If yes, what makes you different or better?)

No, most of the artists I'll film won't have videos online. There's a definite gap in the market for a YouTube channel because I am part of this music scene, and I know there's a demand for more video content.

7. When are you planning to do this?

I can start now. Although if it makes sense to upload a video when that artist is just about to release a new mixtape (to help get more hits/views), I will do that.

8. What are your long-term goals?

I want to become a YouTube partner within three years, as it will increase the money I make from advertising. I want to get a million views on my channel within two years.

9. How will you reach your long-term goals?

I will do this by using the network I have built up in real life and on social media channels, by promoting the artists cleverly (not spamming), and by setting the home screens of PCs at my school and in local libraries to SB.TV ;)

10. How much money do you need? (if relevant)

My business has very low overheads and YouTube is free so the main cost will be my time.

I know it's probably easier for me to do this now looking back, but that's my business right there. So answer those same questions now for your idea or business, and see if it breaks it down and makes things a little more simple. It should help you work out what you need. What's the thing you need most right now? Is it time, skills, money or more people?

DECISION POINT

Now it's time to make a choice as you head into Stage 2 of *The Knowledge*. It's time to think about YOU: looking at yourself as if you were a brand, figuring out what you want and selling yourself in the right way. What do you want to figure out first?

What do you bring to the table?   p 77

Is this a hobby or a career?   p 81

STAGE 1: FIND PEOPLE TO WORK ON YOUR IDEA

When you're really excited about an idea – or you wake up one day and think, 'Yes! I want to start a record label!' – it's tempting to jump in and start finding people to work with straight away. I get that, because I'm kind of impatient, I just want SB.TV to get bigger and better, and to raise my personal profile.

I think before you hire people, you need to know what you're hiring them *for*. Because ideally you want to hire people who fill in the gaps that exist in you. If you're no good at networking, you're going to need a networker. And identifying those gaps is what will make your team strong and rounded, so you can face any challenge. So it's worth taking the time to work out how your idea or business is actually going to function – who is going to be in charge of what? How much will it cost you? Will you need to get a part-time job to fund your idea?

You also need to know as much as possible about the industry you want to work in – from what skills or training you might need, to how to price your product. If you're on your job and you know your game, you'll have a much easier time explaining your vision to your future team. Because you don't want to hire a load of people too early and then risk them asking you 'What's next?' if you don't know the answer. You need to *lead*.

I also think it's good to look at yourself and understand your weaknesses before you start. When I got arrested for ABH after a stupid moment when I totally lost it, that was a massive wake-up call for me because I had time to reflect and think about what I wanted my life to look like. I thought about what kind of person I wanted to be when I got out. I didn't have a choice about taking a time-out because I was in a cell, but you do have a choice. So before you embark on your journey you need to look to yourself and see what skills you have – and more importantly, which ones you lack – because those are the things you might have to 'buy in' down the line. Don't focus too much on beating others – challenging and beating yourself is much more rewarding.

I'm gonna send you back to the Decision Point on **p 66**, where you can choose to make a plan or research your idea.

STAGE 1: START RESEARCHING YOUR IDEA

I want you to research your idea, because it's important to work out the best, cheapest and fastest way to get information about the industry you wanna work in. For example, if you want to write computer software, you need to find out as much as you can about what kind of software the industry use, where you can learn how to use it, how long that's gonna take and how much it costs. You'll want to talk to and network with loads of people who work for software companies; you need to know all the new technologies and which companies offer work experience so you can apply before anyone else. And because it's so competitive, you need to start as young as you can, or if you come to it later, make sure you sell all the skills you've got that are going to fit with what you want to do.

If you've decided to start a business, you need to know what other people charge for products similar to yours, or how their production line works. Then you can improve on what they're doing, do it better and start to beat them at it!

Get out there, NOW

The quicker you find out what it's really like out there in the world, the better. For me, this meant starting SB.TV while I was at college. Then I had a ready-made career and job to jump into by the time I'd finished with education. I'd put in all this hard work while I was still at school, and that bought me the freedom to do what I loved when I left. I was ready, so I didn't go to university, but a lot of my friends did.

If you need to go to uni to make your idea happen, make sure you're doing it for the right reasons. When I hear people say they went to uni because of all the parties and shit, it's ridiculous, because I still did all that stuff regardless, even though I wasn't at uni. Even now, when the freshers come up to London each year I still go to all the parties. I think it's ridiculous when people say, 'Yeah, I just came to uni for the night life,' forgetting that because of those parties, they're in thirty grand of debt. Obviously that doesn't apply for all careers, like medicine or law, which you have to study at uni to practise.

Also if you're gonna spend that kind of money, it's worth sitting down and working out what else you could buy with it. Like, whose time could you buy for thirty grand? You could probably buy Richard Branson's time for that money, or get a one-to-one with an expert in your field. Also if you're smart and cheeky enough, there's a lot of information you can get *for free*. All I'm saying is that I think people should be mindful about university and not think that it's the only way. My education was partly at college and partly just through meeting people who worked in music. Because I was always there, at clubs and on the scene, I learned so much. I also did my research by doing a work experience placement at the BBC. And I networked like crazy. Like I said in Level 1, whatever industry you want to work in, you have to Be There.

Also remember that if you're young, you can get away with more. People are willing to help you if you say you're at college – it makes them feel good to give out advice. So you should work that. Also, like in the first challenge, don't be afraid to be cheeky. You know how many emails people get these days, so yours will have to stand out, even the subject line. Make people laugh because when you email someone, you want it to jump off the page. Sometimes when I email big bosses I put smiley faces in them, because I want people to remember my email over the other 10,839,473 they got that day.

I don't think there's any substitute for practical experience of an industry, because you need to learn the reality of that world. But obviously there are other things you can do in the meantime, to arm yourself with knowledge. If you haven't already, try the following:

- Get a library card. Libraries are like free office space when you start any kind of business.
- Find out which companies do work experience placements. Don't wait until you're nineteen to apply. They'll respect you more if you apply when you're really young.
- Ring people in the field you want to work in. Ask them what training they did to get their job, if any.
- Learn how to Google properly, using the advanced search function. You want to be able to research stuff as quickly as possible, so you can go back to doing what you do.
- Find the best YouTube tutorials you can. You can teach yourself web design, social media, marketing, sound engineering, Photoshop, how to pitch for funding – pretty much anything, online.
- Research internships. Be careful though. Try to at least get your expenses paid and make sure they don't go on for a year without a job at the end of it.
- Learn a new skill or a new thing every day. Give yourself twenty minutes to do it – maybe watch a tutorial online. Do you know what things like 'net profit' mean? Maybe that is your first day's task, to find out.

DECISION POINT

Time to move on to Stage 2. This is about looking at yourself as if you were a brand, and selling yourself in the right way. So it's time to make a choice. Where do you want to go to next?

What's your story?   **p 84**

How much do you cost?   **p 87**

STAGE 2: WHAT DO YOU BRING TO THE TABLE?

One of the most important things you need to do if you want to get an idea off the ground is to know where the gaps in your knowledge are. Before you hire anyone or create a team, you need to have a really solid picture of what you're good at, and what you lack. Are you gonna have to hire someone to make your website, or will you have time to build it yourself? You also need to know what you're best at, so you can spend the most time doing that thing.

It's not all about the £££

If you don't have much money or cool equipment, remember that everyone has to start somewhere. I think your story is really important, because people have always responded to mine and understood that there was a real kid, with a specific skillset, behind SB.TV. Let people grow with your story.

It's OK if your equipment is cheap. If I had been a fifteen-year-old boy with sick equipment, I wouldn't have known what to do with it and my story wouldn't have had the same impact on people. Because they responded to the fact that I did what I did regardless of my cheap camera. I did it because I loved music, and I was never gonna let cheap equipment stop me. And that's why people have grown with my story right from the beginning.

I also never had loads of money pumped into SB.TV. Kids these days are way more advanced than I was when I started off. Back in the day you wouldn't see a kid running around everywhere, filming everything. But now it's OK. So let people grow with your story and if your budget is only like, ten pounds or whatever, stick to that budget. Don't think you have to give in and don't think you have to prove yourself to anyone. If it makes you happy, it makes you happy.

Take positive feedback and constructive criticism and that, but don't let it distract you. If you always work with the attitude that, 'If I don't have the latest equipment, then I can't do it,' then you'll never do anything. Work with what you have and be proud of it, man.

Learning the ropes

If you work out that you're going to need some training or practical experience then get a part-time job and save up, if it means you get to do a work placement. Everyone worked for free at SB.TV at first – presenters, cameras, editors, bloggers, everyone – until we started getting more paid jobs. In the beginning we weren't getting paid to interview people so obviously that wasn't going to make us money. But then it got to a point where the least I could do was pay people's expenses, like food and travel. So I started doing that and then gradually, as I started bringing in more projects, SB.TV could start to pay people wages.

Internships are generally for a longer period. I know most normal kids like me can't afford to work for free for a long time – especially in somewhere like London. But if you need to get work experience and see how your competitors are doing things, internships are a really good idea.

I think it's important to have a time limit on how long you're going to work for nothing – whether it's three to six months, or even a year. Speak to your employer first and ask them to agree to review it after a certain amount of time, if you hit your targets or get their business to the next level. Or even just ask them to start paying your expenses like food and travel after you've proved yourself for three months.

Sometimes I see people doing an internship for a year and then, at the end of the year, I'm like, 'What are you doing, are you going to get paid, are you going to get an actual job?' And that's why I think you need to be upfront at the start of your internship and ask for a review.

I could have done work experience for free for ages, but I was on it, I asked to have a review regularly. And then they can't take the piss out of you, they have to be straight. I think a lot of young people go into internships for *years* and I'm like, 'WHAT? When are you going to renegotiate it? You must be good if they've kept you on for years?'

You have to mention it early on, as soon as you get there. That's what I'm saying – be straight up with your employer, say 'Right, in six months, we're gonna discuss when I'm gonna start getting paid.' The least your employer can do is give you travel expenses. At *least*. One thing you gotta realise about internships is that every day, you're gonna need to get lunch. And if it's not covered by your employer, you're losing money. Every day you get the Tube or bus, you're losing money. So you need to at least keep your receipts and claim your money back, because otherwise at the end of it you might be a grand in debt just from an internship – even though you're getting all that work experience. It's very important to get your expenses covered.

Who do you think you are?

Now I want you to be honest. Really honest, about the kind of person you are, and what you're good at. Not in a 'I'm good at maths' kind of way, I mean, 'Am I good at talking to people?' Because if you are, that probably means you'll be good at marketing your idea and networking to find contacts.

Think about your personality and how you've acted in your life. Forget about what your school or work says you're good at for the minute. Are you the kind of person who organises big nights out for all your friends? Then maybe you should be in charge of strategy for your idea. Are you really on top of current fashion or design, do you cook mad new things, or can you draw? Then you should probably be in charge of your idea's creative department, doing the posters, business cards and logo. Are you good at finding bargains or working out how much everyone owes at Nando's? Then maybe it should be you in charge of numbers, and working out how much to charge people for your product.

When you're done, it should be clear which things you should be in charge of, and which things you're either going to have to bring in to make your idea happen, or ask people to do for you.

DECISION POINT

OK, now it's time to make a decision. How are you feeling? Are you starting to get support from your friends? Do you need some expert help? Let's move on to Stage 3, which is about making sure you've got good vibes around you, and you're getting the right support. Choose the path that represents where you're at.

Your mates don't get it　　　　　　　**p 90**

You want to find people on your wavelength　　　　　　　**p 92**

STAGE 2: IS THIS A HOBBY OR A CAREER?

How big are you thinking?

Before you put your time and money behind an idea, you need to work out what it is. By that I mean, 'Is this idea scalable?' A scalable idea is something that has the potential to grow, and keep on growing – which might mean selling your idea, product or service outside your area, maybe internationally. Or if you're thinking big business, maybe you'll want to work with a 'franchise' model, where your business is set up to have offices all around the world.

If you're thinking about making a product, you need to work out how many people will potentially buy it. So if it's a magazine, and you're selling it for two quid a copy, you need to work out how many you'd have to sell to make a profit, and if there is enough demand for your magazine that people would buy it again, or just on special occasions.

For SB.TV, I knew that if we did things right, and made great videos, people would come back again and again to see whatever we were broadcasting. People don't suddenly stop listening to music or TV, it's a presence throughout their whole life. That made us appealing to brands who wanted to get their stuff in front of young people who watch TV online, and also advertisers, who would pay us money so they were featured in adverts before our videos.

But if you've got a small, more gimmicky item it will be different. If you're making a mobile phone cover, you have to remember that a) not everyone buys one and b) they may only buy one per phone. You also have to remember that there are millions of covers already on the market. So your mobile phone cover would have to be pretty special to stand out and be the one people choose to buy. That's not impossible, of course, but it'd be a harder business to make a profit from than one where you knew there was a massive demand.

You need to think about how often people will need your idea in their life, and if the people who will want it have a lot of money to spare. If nobody else is making your product, it's cheap enough and there's a proven need for it, you'll probably be OK.

What does this mean to you?

OK, you need to figure out early on – like, now – what you're wanting to get out of this. If you bought this book to up your confidence and get tips for knowing how to approach people, or for getting your opinions and ideas out there, then you can treat this as a hobby – something to try – and hopefully give you some self-belief.

Maybe you want to use your idea to make a little extra income, but not necessarily enough to live on. You could say I started out that way. But I could only make it a full-time business because SB.TV was scalable; there was a market out there we could work within, and a proven business model in advertiser-funded TV.

So now you need to do some more research and think about your idea in very, very practical terms. Ask yourself some questions like the ones below:

- How many times in their life would the average person need my idea?
- Could my idea attract government or charitable funding (e.g., Prince's Trust or educational projects like

Shine)? Or could I get financial backing via crowd sourcing?

- How much can I charge for my idea and how much profit will this make me?
- How long will it take me to make my product or organise my event/service?
- How many other organisations or companies are doing or selling this thing?
- Is my idea affected by things like the recession (will people buy it even if they are watching their wallets)?
- What are all the costs associated with my idea (postage, manufacture, transport, technology, equipment)?

Once you've done that, you should have a better understanding of whether your idea is 'scalable' and if it could eventually pay your bills. You also need to think if it's something you could stomach doing day in, day out. Do you have enough fire for this to make it your whole world?

DECISION POINT

And now it's time to make a choice as you move on to Stage 3. You need to get the right support around you, so have a think about what you're looking for. Do you want to:

Find a mentor   p 94

Find someone to sort out the money   p 97

STAGE 2: **WHAT'S YOUR STORY?**

It used to be the case that people didn't care who they were buying stuff from. But now people care about their products – they want to know who's behind the brand or charity or company they buy into and what their story is. So you have to show that. People care about the content creators, they're asking 'Who's behind this?' I don't know why that's happened but it has.

But when you think about some large companies, it's really hard to name the person at the top of the tree. I didn't want to do that so from the beginning, I made sure people knew that SB.TV = Jamal Edwards. It's the same with Richard Branson: people know who he is and what kind of a person he is, and they connect with that. I always want people to notice me too, but not in a way where it's thrown in their face. And now, when I do new things people come along for the ride with me. SB.TV is not a faceless business.

You need to think about yourself in the same way. I think that everyone connects with me because they know my story, and it's something they can tap into. So you should have a story behind what you're doing and why you're doing it, and you need people to know what that story is.

Promoting yourself

Branding is all about telling stories, so if we're talking about you as a brand, it's about selling all your skills and all the great things about you. Everyone's got a story, so don't be afraid to scream and shout about who you are. Because at some point, you're going to need to contact people you don't know – either to advertise what you're doing or to try to persuade them to share your vision.

The thing is, you only really get one shot at this. If someone comes across you online or sees your CV, you don't get long to make an impact. They may only look at your info for seconds, so you have to communicate what you're about in a really punchy way. There are loads of ways to do this. I want you to try one of the following...

Make a visual CV

Instead of writing your CV with words, try using pictures and logos instead. Check out About.me for this. If I was making a CV like this I would put my name, number and email in the middle of the picture and then surround it – like a spider diagram – with the logos of the companies I've worked with or for (BBC, Puma, MTV), and then all the logos of the software I know how to use, like Logic or QuickTime or Final Cut.

You could also just have pictures to represent what you're good at – like a graphic of a computer, if you know how to write code. Though you might still need to label sections so people know what they represent – your skills, your experience, what you want to do. The idea is to tell your story in a way that doesn't need words, so someone only needs to look at your Visual CV to understand what you've done and what you know how to do.

Upload your CV online

There are loads of sites you can use to do this, and you'll need to choose the one which the majority of people use in the industry you want to get into. There are sites that allow you to create an interactive, infographic-style CV, like Vizify. If you want something simpler, you could use About.me, which is more like an online business card.

DECISION POINT

OK, now it's time to make a decision. How are you feeling? Are you starting to get support from your friends? Do you need some expert help? Let's move on to Stage 3, which is about making sure you've got good vibes around you, and you're getting the right support. Choose the path that represents where you're at.

Your mates don't get it   **p 90**

You want to find people on your wavelength   **p 92**

STAGE 2: HOW MUCH DO YOU COST?

One of the hardest things about running a business or organisation is when you have to work out how much to charge for it. The first time I was asked for my hourly or daily rate, or someone wanted to know how much we charged for a video shoot, I had no clue what to say. So I went on the Internet and researched how much camera operators are paid per day in TV, and then I factored in the cost of using our equipment, and how much things like travel were, and then I added a profit margin. That way we covered all our costs and made a profit.

It's also important to know that your time is worth something. Because if you have specialist knowledge or a niche skill and someone wants to hire you (and your brain) because of that, then that should mean they pay you. Even when you do something you love and you're having loads of fun. If you do something you love, you'll never work a day in your life. Because it won't feel like work. That's what I want you to aim for.

Know your worth

The most basic way to price up your time is to first work out how much you cost as a person. It's going to sound a bit crazy, but I want you to think about yourself in terms of how much money is spent on you, day-to-day. How much do you cost to feed, heat and house? What gadgets do you need? Do you go out raving? Do you use any technology?

Start by making a list of all the ways you cost money per month or per year, even if it's not you that's currently paying for this stuff (because one day you'll have your own place, and you will be):

- Food
- Transport
- Phone/Computer
- Internet/Cable
- Clothes
- College/Education
- Fun/Socialising
- Rent
- Council Tax
- Heat and Light
- Water

Basically, include any costs you incur, as long as they are necessary costs in order for you to live to a reasonable standard. And do a reasonable amount of raving :)

Once you have that number, you need to divide it by the number of working days in a month or year (depending on how you worked it out). In 2013 there are 253 working days, so:

How much I cost to run each month (£ ___) ÷ Number of working days in each month (21.08 days) = £ ___ per day.

Or

How much I cost to run each year (£ ___) ÷ Number of working days in each year (253 days) = £ ___ per day.

This figure is how much money you need, per day and AFTER TAX, just to break even. That's how much you cost. And that's before we've even thought about the costs you might run up if you were to start a business – things like stock or manufacturing. It's a solid jumping off point, and a really useful thing to know, whether or not you are trying to set up a company or launch a product.

Putting a price on your skills

If you're going to charge for your time per day/hour you need to take into account how much your specialist skills should cost to buy. Because if you don't have certain experience you will cost less than people who have unusual, creative or more in-depth experience than you. If you're an illustrator or a dress-maker, you can make good money because not everybody can do those things. So you need to add a profit margin that takes into account your specialist skill.

For SB.TV I had to do research on the Internet on how much film crews and editors cost per day/hour, so I could get a guide on this. As long as you make sure you're not getting into debt, though, you should be OK. Also remember that when you start out and you're less skilled, you'll want to charge less than someone who has like twenty years' experience. So be honest about what you can offer if someone wants to hire you, and price yourself fairly.

DECISION POINT

And now it's time to make a choice as you move on to Stage 3. You need to get the right support around you, so have a think about what you're looking for. Do you want to:

Find a mentor   **p 94**

Find someone to sort out the money   **p 97**

STAGE 3: **YOUR MATES DON'T GET IT**

If you've started on this journey and read Level 1, you'll already be doing some things that might draw attention to yourself – in a good way. This can be when things start to get tricky, and maybe your friends and family notice the change in you, and wonder who this new version of you is. Why are you bigging yourself up online? Why do you think you deserve to have your own website?

This is really common, and it can be hard to know when you're on the right track and when it's OK for you to start getting excited about what you're doing. It can be hard for you to know when the buzz you feel is justified.

I think I knew I was headed in the right direction when I got the YouTube partnership, because that kind of validated what I was doing with SB.TV. It meant I was being recognised by YouTube for my videos because of the number of people who were seeing them. That's when I thought, 'All right, I'm doing this for a cause now, because I'm gonna be able to start paying my way from it.'

When that happened it meant I could support myself – which was a big thing for me, in terms of knowing I was doing a good thing. People had started to come up to me on the street and say, 'We like your videos,' and that was equally important. Because it's all right getting paid for something, but if you're not getting respect from the people who you made that thing for, it's not enough.

By then the right kind of people had started queuing up to get on to SB.TV and that showed me I was doing something right, and that was one of the most important things. It's like,

I was always a pretty popular kid at school and I always had friends who would keep up-to-date with what I was doing. But this was different, these were people who I *didn't know*.

Things change, but life doesn't stop

If your friends aren't supportive or they think you're getting above yourself, that can be really hard. Sometimes the first person to get ambitious in any group of friends is going to stand out. And it might make your friends wonder why they're not doing something they really want to do. But you have to remember that people find change difficult – even when it's happening to other people.

If you've spent your life messing about and getting into trouble, it will twist their minds to see you suddenly fix up and make something of your life. But in a way, that's a sign too – because if people are noticing a change in you, you must be having some kind of impact, and you should be proud of that. If that's happening to you, stay in your lane, and don't worry about it.

To stop you thinking about negative stuff I'm going to send you back to the Decision Point on **p 80** (if you came from What Do You Bring to the Table?) or **p 86** (if you came from What's Your Story?) to choose another option.

STAGE 3: YOU WANT TO FIND PEOPLE ON YOUR WAVELENGTH

By now, you should have already established what skills you might need to keep in mind when you're looking for people to work with. When I started SB.TV I was doing everything myself, but that's not to say that as the business has grown I haven't needed help from other people in the music industry or other digital pioneers. You have to find your peers, even if it's just to swap stories of funny stuff that's happened when things go wrong.

But even if my mates hadn't been into grime, I learned early that it's good to engage with other people online, and find your peers that way. Because you want to surround yourself digitally and in real life with like-minded people who get you. I was on every single social network under the sun when I started out. It was busy. And that definitely helped with what I was doing because I worked out how to get people interested. I'll keep hammering that one at you!! I was on Every Network As Soon As It Appeared.

The point is that when you're working on a project on your own, it can sometimes be tough. If I was the only one in the house up at 4 a.m., because I was working on editing a video, it was good to be able to reach out to other people. And if none of your friends or family are into the same thing as you, you'll need to find support elsewhere.

You don't need me to tell you that there's a website and a forum for everything now. But I do want to tell you to get on it, and start making friends with other people who do what you do. You'll then have a ready-made focus group for anything you produce, you'll be able to bounce ideas off them, and help them back. Think of it like laying the foundations for your launch. And then when you come to reveal your vision, you've already got a network of people ready to big you up and shout about how great you are.

Once you've done some networking, I want to know how it went so hit me up on Twitter @selfbelievers and tell me all about it.

DECISION POINT

Well, you're heading to the end of Level 2, so how do you think that went? You feeling positive and ready to shout about it? Choose a path below depending on how you feel it went.

Boom! Success   **p 98**

OK, but I might need to try again   **p 99**

Oh my days it was bad   **p 101**

STAGE 3: FIND A MENTOR

What do you need a mentor for?

Finding someone with experience who you can call upon is kind of vital if you're going into an industry that no one you know has worked in before. It's not like anyone in my family was running an online TV channel! So although I asked my mum and dad for advice a lot of the time, sometimes I was having to decide on business deals for SB.TV that they couldn't advise me on. So back in the day, I made some of the decisions and did some deals without really knowing if I was making the right choices.

For example, some people say I should have got more for certain deals. But I just did the deals, and I didn't really go to anyone and say, 'Is this enough money?' – I negotiated it all myself. But I still stand by those decisions. I told them what I would do and how much it would cost, not knowing what people's budgets were. Sometimes that's a mistake because my rule is that you should never, ever give someone a price before you've found out what their budget is.

At the end of the day, I just did those early deals in good spirit, because I didn't just want to ask for a ridiculous amount of money and then have them think I was taking the piss. And although some people think I might have undersold myself, some of those deals led to good working relationships, so in the end, the decisions were good ones.

Saying that, I also know that there are some decisions I couldn't have made without my mentor, Charlie. I was lucky in that I met him through my mum when she was doing *The X Factor*, and he's been a massive help to me in the last few years, as SB.TV got bigger. Now if anything comes up I can bounce it off him, and get his opinion. I still have control over what I do but he helps me. It's not a weakness to get a second view on things, and you don't have to do what they say, but you do get to see all problems from all angles.

How do I find one?

If you want to find a mentor then you'll need to do a bit of work to prove that you're willing to work with them (or for them) in return for their advice. So you could think about doing an internship with someone in return for them becoming your mentor. Some people will do it out of the goodness of their own heart, especially if you're only going to call on them from time to time – but it's good to have something in your back pocket that you can offer them in return. If you're good at using social media, you could offer to run their Twitter channel in exchange for mentoring.

You also need to think about how you write to them and give them a reason to be your mentor, especially if they've never done it before. If you're going to write to them, and you don't know them, make sure you do loads of research first. Don't say, 'I want you to be my mentor.' Show you respect their experience and then be clear about the ways they could help you. Make a case for why you need the help you do, and how much it would benefit you. Keep writing until you find someone who gets your vision and wants to be involved. You'd be surprised how many generous people there are out there.

The other option of course is to ask someone you respect from within your circle. It might be a tutor or someone in your family – ask someone who's on their job and whose opinion you respect. If you're running a business, it makes sense for your mentor to be in a similar industry, because then when you go to them with a problem they'll probably have had experience of that too.

The most important thing to remember is that it's OK to ask for advice. I see the big bosses doing it all the time and they don't act like they're embarrassed to do it. If you ask questions, you get answers, and you're going to need that knowledge to move forward.

DECISION POINT

We're nearly at the end of *The Knowledge*! I want you to assess how you've done – and be straight with yourself. How did it go?

Boom! Success	**p 98**
OK, but I might need to try again	**p 99**
Oh my days it was bad	**p 101**

STAGE 3: **FIND SOMEONE TO SORT OUT THE MONEY**

When you start any kind of company or organisation you come across people who get all serious and start trying to scare you about things like doing tax, or the fact that you need a lawyer. Don't get me wrong, I have people doing accounts and contracts for SB.TV now, but for the first few years all that side of things was just a myth. It didn't happen.

What I'm saying is that when you start out on your journey, there's no point getting too bogged down in that. Get yourself on the ground and start building the vision. Don't spend loads of money on a whole load of suits or whatever, before you make decisions.

You also need to know that in terms of tax, when you start a company, it's actually really simple maths. Anyone can do it, and you can go on free courses if you're thinking about becoming self-employed, which tell you exactly what you have to do if you need to fill out a tax return.

Obviously there will come a time when you do need these experts. But we're only at the knowledge stage of your vision, so hold off for now. It's not a bad idea to do a bit of research to see who's out there – then if something tricky comes up with money or legal issues, you know who to call.

Right now though, you're still laying the foundations, so don't panic, don't let anyone scare you into thinking that running a business is really hard. I did it, and if I can, so can you. For now, just concentrate all your energy on this idea of yours.

Now let's go back to the Decision Point on **p83** (if you came from Is This a Hobby or a Career?) or **p89** (if you came from How Much Do You Cost?) and try an option you CAN do at this stage.

END OF LEVEL 2: BOOM! SUCCESS

OK everybody, it's time to take a breath and celebrate. If you've completed two levels, you're already a third of the way there. That is great, man, you've earned the right to have some fun before we do Level 3.

I also think now's a good time to take stock and look at how far you've come, because we've covered some pretty big stuff already. If you've done all the tasks in this level, then you'll already be familiar with how to network, and how to plan and research an idea. Most people in full-time jobs don't push themselves to do that sort of thing, ever. You could be way ahead of people much older than you, maybe even your parents, and you might not even be out of school. That is something.

If you've come this far and still feel positive that's also amazing. If you're getting some positive responses to your vision then that's a good sign for the future. I wanna know how it's going, so tweet me @selfbelievers because it'd be cool to know if this book has inspired you to do something.

Head back to the start on **p 57** if you want to try some different challenges, or go to **p 103** and I'll see you in Level 3!

END OF LEUEL 2: OK, BUT I MIGHT NEED TO TRY AGAIN

If you chose this option as the last path in the level then you've probably had a bit of a mixed experience: you're not sure if you're doing well, or maybe the things you tried in this level didn't all end in success. If that's the case, then it's good to get it clear in your head now. What is it that you think you didn't do well? Would you tackle one of the tasks differently this time? Do you still find it hard to talk or write to people you don't know? Are you still feeling shy about talking about your idea online?

Now's the time to identify what it is that makes you uncomfortable because if you push on to Level 3 without thinking carefully about this you'll come up against the same problems. It's great you're spotting things so early you feel a bit unsure of – a bit of extra time looking back on the path you've taken through this level will help you when you take the next steps.

If support is an issue then you should find someone to talk to – whether it's a tutor, work colleague or someone in your family. You could even think about asking your mum or dad for a meeting. I know that sounds a bit crazy but I think any parent would be impressed if you said you wanted to talk to them about what you'd tried, to see if they could help. Having another pair of eyes on a problem is never a bad thing, and I'd have gone mad if I didn't have people to bounce ideas off.

If it's just that you're just not really feeling your idea, then now would be a good time to check it's definitely The One. You feel it in your gut when you hit on the idea that's really going to keep you interested for a long time. So you might wanna try brainstorming to see if you have another idea you could try these *Self Belief* levels on.

Go back to **p 57** and give yourself another run through this level – try different paths this time and see if you can get any more tips or ideas to boost you.

Main thing is, stay positive. It takes time to figure out what path you're on, so go easy on yourself and look at all the great work you've done so far. When you're ready I'll see you on **p 103** for Level 3!

END OF LEVEL 2: **OH MY DAYS IT WAS BAD**

OK, I never said it was gonna be easy! Steadily building the vision is difficult, man. But don't be too hard on yourself, because once you've learned from a mistake, you hardly ever do it again.

Maybe you contacted someone and they weren't interested; maybe you had some knock-backs when you were trying to find a mentor or joined an online forum. Be cool, though, because this is totally normal. If I stood still for long enough to rake over all the stupid stuff I'd done when I was a kid, I'd be messed up.

The best thing to do when you feel like you've failed is to laugh. Go and tell your best mate about what you did and how jokes it was. Tell it like it's a terrible story, laugh at yourself and fix up, because things go wrong all the time out there in the world. The sky hasn't fallen on you; you just maybe embarrassed yourself. It's cool.

If you feel like you want to do this level again, you can go back to the beginning on **p 57**. If not, and when you're ready, swing by for Level 3 on **p 103**. And remember, it's not bad to attempt something and fail. The only bad thing is not to try it in the first place.

BUILDING THE FOUNDATIONS

Level 3

FOREWORD

One of the first things Jamal said when we met him was, 'Chase the dream, not the competition,' and we've never forgotten that. We walked into his Central London office like kids in a candy shop, in awe of the company he had built.

For people like us who are looking to develop a similar business in the digital/new media space, it's incredibly exciting and inspiring to see what he's achieved. He's created this incredible environment that is always buzzing with young and creative people.

Jamal is very focused and switched-on, he's an expert in an area that most people are still trying to get their heads round. He is the guy we bounce ideas off and get advice on growing our business, and with this book lots more people can get some of that advice too.

We hope it helps others as much as Jamal has helped us.

Finn and Jack Harries, JacksGap, 2013

BUILDING THE FOUNDATIONS

INTRO

I hope you're starting to feel a bit more confident about getting to where you want to be. We're at a point in the journey where you've got to stick your neck out a bit, so people know who you are and what you're about.

In Level 3, you'll tap into how to get people to back you up, learn how to deal with people who might be down on you, and figure out how to be IN CONTROL. If you're doing this to get a business idea or a cool project off the ground, then you'll learn some skills for marketing, getting people to invest in your idea, knowing how to work social media, and getting on top of your PR.

Once you've got your foundations right, you can build a whole city, but if you skip on this it'll all crash down on your head. I'm being straight with you: run before you can walk and you'll fall flat on your face.

So, you with me? Let's do it.

MY STORY

Things got a bit mad at Topman, because people were coming in while I was working on my shift; they were asking me about doing videos for them, because they'd heard about me. I needed that part-time job and I really worked hard, but I knew it would get to the point where trying to edit and film videos would clash with the job.

To keep things going I was editing before work, and then after work I would go and film more. It was alright money and some days I'd have off, so I could work on SB.TV; it was a part-time job and I'd been there a while, so I could negotiate that. Most days I was in college; sometimes I'd finish early and work on SB.TV. And then on Sunday I would do an 8-hour shift at Topman, and go out filming after that, then I'd mix it, edit it and upload on Monday morning.

Because I knew I had to keep doing my part-time job and going to college, and wanted to make SB.TV happen, I always found a way to balance it. I left Topman when I realised my heart wasn't in it any more. I was making enough money to keep me going while I gave SB.TV a push to try and make it big-time.

I weighed it all up. I was lucky because I didn't have to pay rent or for anything at home – so all I needed was money for clothes, food and tapes. As long as I had enough to cover that, I was going to make SB.TV happen.

THINGS TO THINK ABOUT

It's really easy to lose that drive you have when you first start out with an idea, like how you felt back in Level 1, especially when you hit the point where you need to get your head down. Think of the number of times you've thought of a great idea – whether it's going to see something, or do something – but you come up with all sorts of reasons not to do it. That's where you need your self-belief voice telling you to keep going.

So this level is about keeping the positivity up and maintaining energy for the launch of your idea – no matter how big or small. Realising ideas takes a lot of energy so make sure you surround yourself with people who give you energy rather than suck it out of you.

Choose the right path for you

If you're just finishing school or college, think hard about what you're gonna do next. One thing I'd say, and I don't wanna slam college or uni, but some of my friends left uni with degrees and some of them are finding it so difficult to get a job. The people I know who got work experience instead are doing well.

So it's like, where's the middle ground? Because the ones with the degree haven't got the experience and the ones with the experience haven't got a degree. So what jump are you gonna take? I would definitely take a gap year. I don't mean like, go to India and hang around for six months. I mean like, get some work experience in the industry you wanna work in, get a taste for it, so you know you're really on the right path, and know what the people in that industry are like. If you decide you want to go to uni then do it – it's just good to know you're doing it for the right reasons, just not because it's what people do. Two of my best mates, Jack and Finn Harries, who did a gap year, now run a channel – JacksGap – with a million subscribers, so you just don't know where it'll take you!

I got to the point in college where I wasn't turning up to lessons, and I wasn't getting the best grades. In some of the lessons, the ones I was interested in, I was good. So it came down to my mum saying, 'Look, do this college thing, get your diploma in Media and Moving Image, and then you can do whatever you want.' I'm glad we made that deal, because that let me get my head around balancing college and what I was starting to do with SB.TV.

Just do it

There's that thing people say, 'If you want something done, ask a busy person.' I think that's true, no question. If I had a video with Skepta and I finished it at 11pm, I would make sure I went home and got it edited that night; I got it done.

I was always dedicated because I knew I had to be to make it happen. I would be editing on my lunch break at college or at work. I've edited in the car, on the bus, on the 266 on the way home – all of that – to get it done. That's what it takes to make things happen: dedication and hard work. It can put a lot of people off, but if you want to do something enough, you'll make the time, you'll find a way.

THE CHALLENGE

OK, so I want you to get back that fire in your belly you had when you started out. You need that dedication to achieve what you're capable of. And now you're about to go out there and start persuading people to be interested in your idea it's more important than ever that you've got your self-belief levels right up.

Whatever your idea is, whatever your passion, you need to give it your time and attention. You can't plant a seed, not give it water and light or whatever and expect it to grow. And this is the same thing. It's time to make sure you're giving enough of you to your idea.

Prove you mean it

You're going to prove your dedication to this by putting aside one hour every day – that's your absolute minimum – to work on your idea. I want you to make a video diary of your progress. Even if it's that you don't get anything done one day – when you see all the video entries, you'll see that you've had loads of days where you achieved so much.

So, figure out what you're going to do in your focus hour. Depending what you're doing, it might be:

- Sitting and writing for an hour a day if you want to write a book, or if you're trying to write an album of songs.
- Spending an hour filming yourself presenting, if you want to be a music presenter.
- Using the hour to research the people that are going

places in the area that you're wanting to get into, and how they've got where they have.

There's no one to check up on you here. I can't stand outside your door shouting at you to get it done!! But you'll know if you're slacking on this, because that great idea you had? Not happening.

Tweet me @selfbelievers and let me know how you're getting on. This is the time to show yourself you've got the stamina and the determination to make it.

DECISION POINT

That focus time is really important. You can spend 12 hours a day doing something but not getting anywhere because you're not using the time in a way that's going to benefit you. Or you can spend one hour getting your head down and making the time work for you.

OK, that's got your brain warmed up, so it's time to start choosing your own path as we head into Stage 1 of *Building the Foundations*. Which one is it gonna be?

Get some public feedback   **p 113**

Give yourself an incentive to keep going   **p 125**

Get a work space   **p 120**

STAGE 1: GET SOME PUBLIC FEEDBACK

So you've got your idea, you've done a bit of research about the area you're working in, now it's time to put it to the test. You wouldn't drive a car that hadn't been road-tested so why should anyone buy into what you're doing if you've not proved it's up to scratch?

Ask the right questions

I'm going to send you out onto the streets in a minute, but first I want you to think about your idea. By now you know who the market is for your idea; if you're selling it you know what price you're wanting it to retail at; you've got a pretty good idea what it looks like and where you're hoping to promote it. But you've not actually asked the big P – the public – what they think about all that. So let's do it.

Step 1

First things first. Get on your computer, or go old school and grab a pen and paper, and I want you to think of some questions to ask people that will really help you get good feedback on your idea. Here are some questions for starters:

- Would you buy into this idea?
  - If not, why not?
  - If yes, what is it that got your attention?

- Who do you think it would most appeal to?
- Do you think the pricing is right? (if this applies)
- Does this have mass appeal or will only a small number of people like it?

Don't ask more than 12 questions or people won't want to help you – when you tell them it'll take a minute, mean it. Really think about your idea, and make sure your questions will lead to answers that help you firm it up and make it better.

Don't cheat – and by that I mean don't ask questions that make the person answer in the way you want them to, like 'Do you think this would look better in red?' You're leading them instead of letting them answer how they would if you just said, 'What colour do you think this should be?'

Step 2

When you're done, type your questions up and leave space for people to answer how they want, or if you've got Yes/No questions put in tick boxes. Then print off 20-30 copies on A4 paper.

Step 3

Now you're ready to hit the streets.* You can either walk up to people near your local shops, or at your nearest park or wherever, or if it's freezing or rainy, hit your local community centre, caf, pub (if you're legal!!), college or wherever there's lots of people who'll give you different points of view. Don't ask your mates/family. This is about the people OUT THERE.

* Always make sure someone knows where you are, and stay in public spaces at all times. If you're 13 or younger, make sure you've got an adult with you.

People who're gonna be honest cos they're not gonna see you again ;)

Give yourself an hour to get feedback, then head home. It's not easy walking up to people, so if you managed to do it, you get proper self-belief points.

What does the feedback mean?

So what did the people you spoke to say? Unless you're really lucky, not everyone will have given 100% positive feedback. If you can take the good comments about what you do, you've got to be open to some of the not-so-good comments too; it's only fair. But it's OK to feel a bit pissed about it, you're human too!! Just feel it, then tell yourself, 'OK, it's cool, what can I take from what they've said?'

When I was posting videos on YouTube, I'd get feedback beneath them. Man, some people just want to troll! But not all negative comments are trolling, and that's what you've got to figure out, which criticism to listen to, and which to say, 'OK, that's your opinion, but it's not going to help me.'

Hopefully you'll have had a mix of good feedback and useful ideas for what you could change. Write down one thing you're really pleased about from this, and one thing you think that you need to change. Use this to shape and improve your idea. The best creative people and business people know that you can ALWAYS improve – there's no such thing as perfection.

DECISION POINT

Now you've got focused feedback and you've stayed true to your vision, you're ready for the next step, which is about putting your stamp on your idea. And yeah, you've got to make a decision! What's your next priority?

Being ready to connect   **p 130**

Smartening up your branding   **p 136**

STAGE 3: PAY FOR AN ADVERT

Woooooooaaaahhh! Slow down. You're getting there with your idea, you're starting to nail down the practical things you needed to get sorted, and you're keeping the energy going to make it to the launch stage (Level 4). That's all sick, and you should be proud. I mean that.

So take a time-out to look at everything you've done and think about what you've got left to achieve. You don't need to be spending your money on an advert right now. Just think about it. If you start putting out that your idea is all ready to go (maybe it's a gig you're wanting to do, a dance class you're setting up, or an online company) when you're not there yet, you're going to look a bit shady when people start calling up or emailing or whatever and you can't give them what they're calling for – no date set for that gig, no venue for that dance class, no products ready for that online company.

When you're ready for it, you'll be using free sites to promote yourself before anything else. You can use media that you've already got – your Twitter account, Facebook, Instagram, Keek – to get your idea out there. Don't start paying people until you're at the point where it's really gonna benefit you.

OK, you've had a breather, done a reality check, so let's take it back to that Decision Point you were at on **p 129** (if you came from Find Out What Makes You Special) or **p 137** (if you came from Smartening Up Your Branding).

STAGE 2: COME UP WITH A NAME FOR YOUR IDEA

With so many top ideas out there you've got to use everything you've got to 'wow' people. And that means as well as a good idea, you've got to get the look right, and give your concept a name that's going to leap out.

I can't count the number of times people ask me what SB.TV stands for man!! It used to stand for Smokey Barz from back in the day when I was out shooting grime vids everywhere. But now I use the SB initials to stand for whatever it is I'm representing, like my motto: 'Self-Belief'.

It's good to think about where your idea's come from, what's your brand story – at this point. It's nice when everything about a brand 'makes sense' and sits right. But to sit right it's got to be authentic, so try to come up with a name which has meaning/a fun explanation behind it, like how SB.TV tells you it's my company, and I used that name even when my stuff was on Bebo, MySpace, YouTube...

Some people will know right off what they want to call their idea. If that's you, make sure you run it past people – hit the street and poll people's response to it. Your mates might worry about upsetting you so it's best to try it on people you don't know so well.

If you go kind of blank when you try to think what to call what you're doing, sit down and write/type out ten words or phrases you think represent what you're doing best. These might include:

- Your main values
- Maybe the name of the place you live if it inspired you

- A motto you think says what you're about
- Something linking to your favourite football club

When you've done that, get online and google those words/ phrases one by one or go to a thesaurus site. Google's good because it'll bring up suggestions that link to the word you've put in, and that might lead to finding the ultimate name for your thing.

It doesn't have to be too specific. It's kind of cool that people are a bit confused by what SB.TV means; the main thing is they remember it because it's snappy. Once the name's in their head, boom!

DECISION POINT

OK, it's time to make a decision and go to the next stage of making your idea happen. Read the choices below, have a think about what you want to do next and pick one of the options.

Sell shares/Let someone use your idea	**p 122**
Market your idea	**p 138**

STAGE 1: GET A WORK SPACE

As SB.TV got bigger, and once I had a bit of a team, a load of us were all working from our own separate homes and communicating online. Sometimes people would come to my house but we'd mostly just do work over emails and phone.

Then it stepped up from just being here, there, everywhere and Starbucks (I had *loads* of meetings in Starbucks) to finding some free space in Camden. The deal was we would mention them in a few videos, and mention them on Twitter, Facebook, whatever, and they let us stay there for a few months. The first office space we paid for was near Latimer Road – and that was 2012.

Where we are now is more of an office. We're in much more of a work environment, which is so much better. Everyone's getting down to work and doing their thing.

I used the YouTube money and invested it back in to us getting a work space – most of the money SB.TV makes I invest back in my business. So as long as we break even, it's alright.

When you get office space together you're not gonna have to wait an hour for someone to get back to you. If I want someone to do something I want to be able to just go over and ask them to do it. Also to the outside world looking in, when we have meetings, it just looks more professional, and it's definitely a step up from the previous set-up.

Make the most of what you've got

You can't spend money you don't have getting the latest iPhone/laptop every time they upgrade. Well, think the same way about where you work on your idea. When you start out you shouldn't be spending money on hiring space to work. Do what you can with what you have.

So if you are working on your idea at home or at college, make sure you've got a space where no one's gonna interrupt you, and – unless you need it for what you're doing – stay away from social media/TV/radio/PSP while you're working!! It's fine when you're taking a break or you're promoting your stuff or whatever, but when you're getting stuff down, you need to keep your focus.

If you live at home with your family, find a bit of the house – even if it's just a table – that you can keep clear for you to go to and work on your idea. Try to make it separate from where you usually chill out. If you've got a local library, they're free to join, so go and hang out there if you need some quiet place to concentrate. Or you might be able to get a desk in college or if you're at work there might be a breakout area you can use to get thoughts down.

DECISION POINT

Once you've got your own space you'll find it a lot easier to concentrate on the things you've got to get done. So if you've got that sorted, it's time to figure out what you need next. Do you want to:

Find out what makes you special   **p 127**

Come up with a name for your idea   **p 118**

STAGE 3: **SELL SHARES / LET SOMEONE USE YOUR IDEA**

Before I wrote this, I hadn't admitted this to people, but I nearly sold off 50% of SB.TV in the early days. Yep, that's right, I nearly gave away half my company.

Stay smart

This is what it's like running your own business or putting something of yourself out there, and why you have to watch out for people who don't necessarily have your back. Especially when you start to be successful, because people will start wanting a piece of you or trying to make deals with you that benefit them more than they benefit you.

There are good things about getting noticed and people wanting to get into what you're doing, don't get me wrong. But you have to be careful. If someone's offering you something for free, there's maybe gonna be a catch.

If it sounds too good to be true, it probably is

Earlier on in my career, one of the things that was helpful is that we used to get free studio time, and we had a partnership with this studio – so like, they could put their logo on my videos in return for giving us free studio time, which was a good thing. You should always try to use local synergies or the right synergies to help you get up, because you can't do everything yourself. Synergies for us was getting access to equipment that at that time SB.TV couldn't afford, so we gave away free advertising on our channel to someone who would let us use their equipment. And you're always going to need someone's help, in some shape or form.

So I made this partnership with this studio, until one day they turned around and had this contract. Basically, I was young, and I had no one around me to ask, and I was kind of in my own bubble so I just thought, 'Oh, this is SICK, I'm gonna get like five grand,' or something. Then because I'd broke my camera they lent me one of their cameras, and so along with the money they were just gonna like *give* me the camera.

I was like, 'Oh my God, this is amazing.' And I was SO CLOSE to like, signing away the majority of my company to them. Which was kind of sneaky. It was mad, because I'd known this guy since school, but it's funny how some people change. He was one of my friends but he came to my house, and he was in this car and he was like, 'This is gonna be brilliant, we're gonna do this, this and this,' and he was really keen for me to sign. And I nearly did. I mean, it was a good thing that I'd survived up until then without getting any legal advice, but that was bare close.

If you're not in business, it can be more of a case of people taking your idea and asking to use it somewhere – like maybe you're an illustrator and someone asks to use your pictures, but you didn't make sure you copyrighted your stuff before you let them have it, so now they can sell stuff with your illustrations on. Whether this is serious business or a fun thing you're proud of, you don't want someone stealing credit for what you're doing.

Think twice

If someone's wanting in on your idea – especially if your idea isn't at a stage where you'd get a lawyer involved or can't afford one – the best thing is to ask your parents, a teacher or someone more senior to you at work who you trust.

I wasn't hooked up with a lawyer then because it was so early – grass roots stages – but this person with the contract obviously saw the potential and tried to make me sign. I didn't, which was lucky.

The thing to remember is that the more someone wants you to sign a contract, the more wary you should be. Nobody should need to put crazy pressure on you to sign a contract – if it's a good deal for you, you won't need to be pressured because you'll want to sign anyway. But this guy, every day he was phoning me and he was giving me stuff like a new camera, and promising me other things. I was like, 'I don't really need anything, bruv, like chill.' But it made me think. 'What's your motive?'

When I said I didn't want to sign they were like, 'But we gave you the STUDIO to borrow, and we helped you out!' But I was like, 'Are you actually serious? You gave me the studio and thanks for that, but I built this up.' I don't really talk to him any more, it wasn't a good look. I can't believe I nearly done that, man.

I told you that so you can learn from my close call. Don't think about the immediate money or the immediate glory of having someone want to share in your idea. Think about the long-term and how you want to have loads of people fighting to be involved with you and your idea, and keep your cool. You'll know if the time's right to share this thing, financially or as a concept.

Let's head back to the Decision Point on **p 119** (if you came from Come Up With a Name for Your Idea) or **p 132** (if you came from Being Ready to Connect) and choose an option that's really going to help you go places.

STAGE 1: GIVE YOURSELF AN INCENTIVE TO KEEP GOING

You know what? Lots of people will tell you not to do this, to keep your head down and only treat yourself when you're doing really well. But you've got to keep yourself motivated. You've gotta know when to push yourself hard, but it's just as important to know when to give yourself a clap.

When I got my first paycheck from YouTube I spent it all in one go. I banked it and went straight across the road to the jewellers and bought myself this ring I wanted. I have a thing about jewellery, especially the stuff Thomas Sabo does with skulls on, so that was what I was going to get myself to say, 'Well done mate, you're making this happen.'

I think it's important to treat yourself to something nice you'll always keep with the first bit of money you make yourself. Every time you look at that thing you'll remember how your own mind paid for it and even if you don't like it years later, you'll still be really proud of what you did.

I don't really buy a lot with my money apart from spending it on taxis and – because I've got a thing about skulls – I've bought like, Alexander McQueen scarves with skulls on them or jewellery. But mainly I spend my money on food and travel. People often say, 'Oh Jamal, you could dress so much better,' but I just think, 'What are clothes doing for me?' You know, what does it prove?

So providing you've made a good start and you're making progress, go for it, treat yourself – but don't go mad and do this all the time. Treat it as a one-off, and only do it again when you know you've properly earned it. Now you've given yourself that incentive to keep going, go back to the Decision Point on **p 112**, which will take you back to make another choice.

STAGE 2: FIND OUT WHAT MAKES YOU SPECIAL

Work out what you want to achieve

This is where experience really comes into play. In terms of knowing what I wanted to do with SB.TV, I knew exactly the kind of people I wanted to film, how many subscribers I wanted, and which record labels I wanted to get in with. And you need that because you've got to set yourself targets to aim for. I didn't put dates on it.

One massively important thing is really listening to people, and being flexible. Take figuring out what to charge people for what you're doing, which can be hard when you start out. I really didn't know so I just used to charge £100-300 for a video, to film it, cover petrol, edit it and get it up. I didn't know if that was low or high or what. I just thought, I need fifty pound for petrol, and the rest of it is just time. I charged that amount for a long time, until it was enough for me to leave Topman and start working on SB.TV full time. So I was then getting the money from YouTube and for making the videos as well.

With some people who were just coming up, I knew they couldn't afford that kind of money, so I charged the more high-profile people and used the money from YouTube to finance the underground people who couldn't afford to use me for a video. I would rather be able to provide a free service for new talent. Then when they hopefully shine off the back of it, in whatever field that they're working, that makes me happy. If I work with brands I obviously charge for that, but for MCs that are coming up I don't charge.

Lesson being, if you're flexible and know who your customers are, and what is right for them, they'll appreciate it. That personal relationship is so important, and it will set you apart.

These days lots of people say, 'It's just business, it's not personal' – but for me, it's *totally* personal. From the people I work with, to the people who are keeping up with what we do. If you engage with people on their level then you'll stand out.

Know your competition

It's cool you know what you want, but when it comes to convincing other people that what you're doing is worthwhile, you've got to know what makes your idea stand out. There's no way of cutting corners here: you've got to do your research. When I say know your competition, I don't mean start trying to copy other people. I mean know what makes you DIFFERENT to them, in good ways. Ask yourself some questions:

- Is anyone out there doing the same thing as you?
- If they are, how is what you're doing different/better?
- Are they targeting all available markets, and if not how are you going to do what they're not?

Whatever you do you've GOT to have an angle: it might be that your idea's cheaper, more creative, better quality, healthier, more specific, whatever. It's got to stand out or you're going nowhere.

Sometimes it needs a fresh pair of eyes to see what it is that makes what you're doing unique. Don't ask someone too biased, like your mates or your family, who'll be like, 'Yeah you're the best!' – you need someone who can look at it with a bit of distance, maybe a teacher or someone you work with who you respect and trust. Listen to their feedback. If it rings true, then they've probably hit on your USP, your unique selling point.

DECISION POINT

Now it's time to think about promoting your idea and getting the word out about what you're doing. So choose a path below and let's move on to the next stage.

Pay for an advert p 117

Write a press release/announcement p 133

STAGE 2: BEING READY TO CONNECT

You'll know pretty well by now where you're at with your idea. Maybe you're starting to get some people interested in what you're doing, or maybe you're realising it's something you just want to do in your own time, and not push it to be a major part of your life. Either's cool – knowing what you want out of this is the main thing.

Whether you're seeing this through in a serious way or on a more fun basis, you still want people to know about your idea. And you can't do that without letting people know who you are and what you're about.

Maybe you're setting up a dance class locally – or maybe this is about letting people know you've got your own company, or maybe you're in a company and want to look professional.

- If you're in a company you can generally get business cards made for you. Be brave! Even if you're at an assistant level, ask whether you can have a card. Say you're planning on doing some networking and make it about how this will be useful for the company. If they think there's something in it for the business, they're not going to say no.
- If this is a personal project, or is for your own company or idea, don't go crazy spending loads of money – this is just so you look more professional when you're networking. It doesn't matter if it's just an A6 sheet of paper with your name/phone/email/Twitter etc. Make it memorable if you can – if you're a clothes designer,

pierce the card with a safety pin and a piece of fabric that represents your look.

Making it personal

I'm always going on about the importance of being visible, of people knowing who you are. Maybe 10 years ago it didn't matter if people didn't know your story, or didn't know who was at the head of a company, but it does now. People want to know they can trust the person behind an idea, that they are on the same wavelength.

Doing flyers or getting business cards shouldn't be about having an identikit card that looks like you work in a bank. It's about getting across who YOU are. So put your social media contacts down, make it look personal and get people to engage with you, as well as your idea.

Find a decent online place that will print them for not too much money, and then once you've got them printed, HAVE THEM ON YOU ALL THE TIME. What's the point in having something that says who you are if you're going to keep it at home?? This is your way of reaching out to someone if you're at an event, or if you're not going to get much time with someone. Worried about what you're going to do with your flyers/business card? Simple. Just do this:

- Introduce yourself.
- Say in a sentence what your idea is.
- Pay them a compliment, nothing creepy, just to make them feel you're hitting them up because you respect them.
- Ask if you can give them your card. DONE.

DECISION POINT

OK, it's time to make a decision and go to the next stage of making your idea happen. Read the choices below, have a think about what you want to do next and pick one of the options.

Sell shares/Let someone use your idea   **p 122**

Market your idea   **p 138**

STAGE 3: WRITE A PRESS RELEASE / ANNOUNCEMENT

You've done your research around what other things are out there, you've figured out what makes your idea different to everyone else's, and you're getting ready to launch it out in the big bad world o_o

Before you do that, you want to give people a teaser of what's coming. This is basically a press release – that might sound a bit full-on if you're just doing this for fun, so call it a promo or announcement if that makes you feel better. Whatever, you need to let people know what's coming. And this is something you can do for free.

What's in it?

All the way through this book, and all six levels, you'll hear me saying the same thing: KEEP. IT. SIMPLE. This promo, this press release, is all about letting people know your idea is about to hit them, so give them the bare details and no more. Keep it short and sweeeeeeet!

- **What is it?** E.g. Gig/fashion label/a presentation of an idea at work/website?
- **Where's it happening?** Online? In real life?
- **When?** What's your launch date? Or when are you going to be presenting your idea?
- **How does it relate to them?** Why do they HAVE to know about it/buy into it?

Who's going to see it and where?

OK, so you know what you want to put in your announcement, and who you want to target – and if you don't by now you really need to go back to Level 2. The main thing here is how you're gonna reach them. If you've got email addresses of people you want to know about your idea, that's great. But don't just fire off a standard email to everyone on your list. Make it personal. Put in their name, mention why you're sending it to them specifically. Flatter them. EVERYONE likes people saying nice stuff about them.

Maybe you haven't got an email database to hit up, so go on social media and find who you want to get to. People think that it's enough just be present on the internet, as if just being on there means that something will happen. I don't know why people think that. You have to draw attention to what you're doing until you find your peers or your audience.

Just posting links to what you're doing on Twitter isn't good enough, it's just loose. You need to talk to other people and support what they're doing if you want them to do the same for you.

There's a really dangerous line between spamming people and getting their attention. You don't want to piss people off or make them bored of you before you've even got started. I would always try to offer people something they'd never seen before – like exclusives of artists they should know about – to get the word out in the early days.

In the beginning I would put a post on every single person's page I wanted to hit up, but I would personalise each one so they knew my post was just for them. I made a status that I could use in lots of different ways. It would have been much easier for me to just ctrl+paste on everyone's page but then they would know that I hadn't put any effort in; I wouldn't have really been connecting with them.

And that's what you have to do. That person felt the message that I had left was just for them, so it wouldn't get deleted. I would say like, 'Hey, that's a cool top in your picture,' or something else nice. You've got to take TIME to do this stuff if you want people to connect with what you're doing. A compliment always helps!

Then you need to get them hooked on your story. If someone wants to get my attention, they first of all have to be good. But I'm mostly interested in people who are conscious, who have a bit of a story behind them. I love conscious rappers because when I listen to their music I feel like I'm on a journey with them. I feel like I'm a part of it too.

The follow-up

The last thing to remember is that you need to FOLLOW UP your press release/e-shot. You need to be on your job. Like, if I keep seeing you at the same events, I'll know you're on your job. I see the same people again and again so I know that they're always there, they're committed. That shows me that they're dedicated. If people want to get my attention in music I want them to take me on a journey. So make that introduction, tell people what you're about, then let them feel it!

DECISION POINT

Now BREEEEEAATTHHHE! You just did a whole lot of good right there. Big up! But how are you feeling? Did you get the results you hoped from putting the message out there? Time to be honest about how things went for you. So how'd it go?

Boom! Success	**p 142**
OK, but I might need to try again	**p 143**
Oh my days it was bad	**p 144**

STAGE 2: SMARTENING UP YOUR BRANDING

I'm not talking about your face or your clothes – I'm talking about how you're presenting your idea. The best ideas are simple and you should be able to pitch it to someone in one sentence.

So first thing to do is, put your idea, your pitch, what you're selling, into a sentence. And not a 500-word sentence!! Then make it ten words max.

Next try it in five words. If you can't keep it snappy you're not going to convince anyone.

Now you've got your idea into a bite-sized pitch, it's time to think about how you're going to present it visually. We're bombarded with photos all the time so we know how important it is to present what we're doing in a slick way.

You might be doing this on a personal level, and not thinking business – maybe you're trying to get people at college to go to some group you've set up or whatever. To persuade people, you need to put across your idea in a way that jumps out at them and says YOU WANT THIS!! It's the same if you're setting up in business or doing a work project. If it looks shabby no one's gonna take a second look.

This basically comes down to branding. You want to look professional, you want to have your own style, your own thing. So, whether you're designing a logo for a company you're setting up or for a product, or whether you're designing a poster to get people to come along to an event, these things are SO important:

- A good advert or a good logo is all about simplicity. It's even better when they communicate what you're trying to do with very few words, or none at all.
- Keep your design to 2-3 colours max, and make sure it's not so busy that your message gets lost.
- Make it memorable. See if you can persuade an arty mate to help in return for a credit on your website.
- Get feedback. You've got to keep doing this all the way through these levels. If you've bought this book it's because you want to get your self-belief up to pitch something to other people. And you can't do that with confidence if you've not got other people's opinions on each stage.

OK, good work. Are you happy with your look? If you're not sure if someone's comment is useful or not, ask the opinion of someone you trust.

DECISION POINT

Now it's time to think about promoting your idea and getting the word out about what you're doing. So choose a path below and let's move on to the next stage.

Pay for an advert   **p 117**

Write a press release/announcement   **p 133**

STAGE 3: MARKET YOUR IDEA

You're probably saying, 'OK Jamal, I get what publicity is but how is marketing different?' Or maybe you already know.

Well, good marketing is all about understanding who your brand will appeal to, knowing where they 'live' whether online or in real life, talking to them in a language they understand, at the right time, and ideally using low cost methods (e.g. social media). Publicity is getting out and shouting your message loud and clear in the right places.

Spread your net to catch more fish

If I'd promoted SB.TV to, like, some classical music outlets, back in the day, I'd have gotten NOWHERE. That sounds obvious, and that's an extreme example, but what I'm saying is, know who you need to reach before you actually put your idea out there.

You're probably clued up on this – if you're passionate about what you're doing, you're most likely going to know the sort of people you want to reach, but that doesn't mean you know everything.

Get online/Google to see if you can find Facebook pages that might be interested in what you're doing; ask people you're already following if they can suggest people to contact in the same area. You might know a lot, but you don't know it all – and don't EVER think you do. That's just lazy.

Finding your people

Reaching people online and in real life is the key to getting any idea out to more people than just yourself and those you see every day.

When you start out, it can be pretty scary talking to people about what you do, especially if you're not this crazy confident person. I knew I had to get my mates to help me promote things, and it's a good way to get started. But when I say your mates, I don't just mean your proper close mates, I mean your Facebook friends, your Twitter followers.

When I started out I was using MySpace and Bebo and Facepic and hi5 and Neopets. I had literally every single social network under the sun and that definitely helped with what I was doing because I worked out how to get people interested in it. I was on Every. Network. As. Soon. As. It. Appeared.

Some of them I just used to talk to people, but I would always be promoting SB.TV or Smokey Barz in one way or another. I would go into chat rooms like BlackChat and just chat to people, lol. Everyone at school was on it, and it was mainly just for people who had beef, but it was funny because we would go on and chat to people and then sign off going, 'See you tomorrow at four!' to people I didn't know at all. We'd meet up like it was the park or something.

Sometimes even now I might bump into someone and they'll be like, 'Oh, I remember you from BlackChat!' Which isn't always so great!! We were just talking about the stuff that teenagers talk about, just rubbish like football and girls, money, everything. It's cool to talk about personal stuff, but remember once it's out there it's OUT THERE. You can take down tweets but people might have retweeted/reblogged/reposted it, and it doesn't always get taken down from all versions of whatever site you're using... So just be conscious what you're saying!

Get a hit list

Put together a list of emails, websites, blogs, Twitter handles, Facebook pages, whatever, in a spreadsheet or a Word doc. Just get it all down in one place. Maybe you need to group it under different headings – 'BIG SHOTS', 'PEOPLE I KNOW'. Then for each heading, you need to write down how you're going to approach them. You can't make a pair of trainers and hope it'll fit everyone – it won't. You know people aren't physically the same, so don't treat them like they're the same when it comes down to their opinions and how they respond to stuff.

Think it through; ask people what they respond to when they get promotional emails, or tweets, whatever. What's a turn-off? What makes them think I want to hear more? What would get a response out of them?

Write everything down:

- Who you're targeting and why.
- How you're going to reach them.
- How you'll make sure you're speaking to them on their level?

Once you've started reaching out to people, make a note of how it's going. All the good stuff and the negative stuff too. Put it in two columns, and make sure you keep it balanced so you don't get ahead of yourself, or too down on yourself. Stay on a level and you can move forward knowing what you're doing right and what you still need to work on.

DECISION POINT

OK, time to check in. How did that go? Did you reach out to the people you needed to? Did you switch it up so you spoke to them in a way they'd get? Depending how it went, go to:

Boom! Success   **p 142**

OK, but I might need to try again   **p 143**

Oh my days it was bad   **p 144**

END OF LEVEL 3: **BOOM! SUCCESS**

Wicked! You've kept your head down when you needed to, did the hard graft, made sure you were hitting the right people at the right time, and it's paid off.

If you chose this option, it means you've got the people that you wanted to be interested in your idea starting to bite. They want to hear more, see more, know more. And you're ready to take it up a level to *Launch Time*.

If you've got a team around you now, it's a good time to go out and celebrate, spend a bit of time together so you know you're all aiming for the same thing and you're all excited about where you're going. With everyone on the same page you're ready to get your idea fully out in the open, for people to buy/watch/read/eat/wear.

It might be a good idea to give this level another go, but take different paths this time so you get to do different tasks and learn other skills. If you think that would help, go back to the start on **p 103** and pick up some more tips.

But if you're feeling ready and want to push on with it, I'll see you on **p 145** at Level 4 ;)

END OF LEVEL 3: OK, BUT I MIGHT NEED TO TRY AGAIN

You're doing good, and don't forget that. This level has been all about not stopping when you hit the point where you need to work hard, about not losing your energy or drive to make this happen. And you've kept that positivity up, and worked your ass off to make sure your idea is ready to be shared with the world.

But I can tell there are things you're not sure about still, you're a bit worried about getting mixed feedback, and your self-belief is wavering a little bit. Go back through the feedback you've gotten on this level. When you've got negative feedback, look at what you've learned from it and how it's helped you shape your idea. If I'd had people just saying, 'Jamal, you're the GOAT' when I started out, I'd never have fixed up and made SB.TV as good as it could be. So take it as a positive – those people were interested enough in what you were doing to give you feedback that could help you move it to a better place. Isn't that better than no one telling you where you could improve?

And if people are just being down on you for no reason? You KNOW you're doing something right. People say stuff about people they're jealous of, or who are standing out.

With the feedback you've got, maybe it would be a good idea to go back to the beginning of this level on **p 103** and see if you'd do anything differently, knowing what you do now.

If you feel ready to move on, keep your head up, stay positive, and I'll see you on **p 145** at Level 4.

END OF LEVEL 3: OH MY DAYS IT WAS BAD

Everyone hits a point in making their idea come to life where they feel like it's just not going their way. Without that roadblock you wouldn't stop to take checks on all the different things you need to make your idea happen.

It might feel like a setback, but if you're getting no feedback, or just negative comments, or people aren't really getting what you're about, this is your chance to sharpen things up. When things go well you've no reason to stop and do an MOT on your idea! But you HAVE got that chance, so look on this as a good thing.

This level was all about keeping your focus, and it sounds like you've found it a bit difficult to keep the energy flowing. But it is still there – you've made it to the end, so you should hold your head up high.

Go back to the start of this level on **p103**, and, using the feedback you had from your first attempt, see what you can do differently. Maybe you need to make sure your idea is easy to get across in a quick pitch. Or maybe you're presenting it in a way that doesn't really represent what you're about. The time you put in at this stage is gonna pay off big time later on, so don't be down on yourself.

This is just a pit-stop. You're checking the engine, and soon you'll be up and out on the track again.

LAUNCH TIME

TIME

Level 4

FOREWORD

When I first met Jamal, we were both nineteen. He was a very quiet, shy guy, but I could tell he knew his stuff when it came to videos and social media, as he already had a large following. We hung out a lot, filmed a lot of live videos of my songs, and went to go and see live concerts of underground artists.

The second video he filmed of me was my song, 'You Need Me I Don't Need You', which we recorded at Sticky Studios in Surrey. This was a song I'd been playing for years without any success, so I didn't really know what would happen once he uploaded it to his SB.TV YouTube channel, but I thought it couldn't hurt. Within a week I had half the urban scene – people I was fans of – getting in contact through Jamal asking to work with me; labels took notice of the views and the hype and it started the ball rolling.

Within a year I signed with Atlantic and now three years later here I am. It all sparked off a chain reaction and I will always remember Jamal for starting that. He has built his company from a cheap video camera and a Wi-Fi connection into a multi-million-pound enterprise covering all bases; underground, pop, rock, interviews, poetry and youth culture. There is no one like him in our industry and I love the risks he takes because every single one has paid off so far.

I don't know what's next with Jamal, because you *never* know what's next with Jamal, but I can guarantee that it's gonna be epic, and I can't wait to see the growth. I owe a lot to him.

Ed Sheeran, 2013

LAUNCH TIME

INTRO

This is the level where it all kicks off and you're going to need to make sure you've done all the legwork to try to make your idea a success.

So, in Level 4 – *Launch Time* – you'll take the route you choose, but some of the things we'll cover include: final checks before launch time for your project, including making sure your self-belief levels are up; keeping the promotional side going – knowing who to contact and how, now your idea is out THERE; and keeping on top of the money side of things.

You up for it? C'mon, let's get going.

MY STORY

The hard-graft days

It took me a few months to set up SB.TV, but years to get it to where it is today. I went through a long time of emailing every singer I wanted to feature, their PRs, managers... And a lot of that time was spent being totally ignored because I wasn't big enough for them to take notice or whatever. I had to prove myself, and I wasn't going to take any knock-backs.

It's easy for people to look at me now and think, 'Oh, he's got it easy – he has access to all these artists.' But man it took AGES to get to that point, and a lot of walls had to be knocked down to get there. You think I'd have got to interview John Legend when I first started out?! Nah. It doesn't work like that and it never will. You've gotta earn people's respect and trust. Prove you've got what it takes, and people will start to notice what you're doing and want to be a part of that.

For the first three years of SB.TV, I was running it all on my own, which is mad to think now. I'd go out and film in crazy situations – going to bits of London where I'd never been before at random times of night to shoot stuff. It was those early vids that started to get people's attention, but it wasn't glamorous!! I had a mate driving me round or I'd get the bus to wherever I was shooting. I remember one time we'd been at a pirate radio station and the local crew turned up in bandanas and balaclavas, trying to bring trouble to us. We split before anything could kick off – it was a case of wrong place, wrong time. So yeah, those early days weren't always easy!

The buzz after SB.TV took off

But it was those first years where I got to shoot leading names in the UK grime scene, like Dizzee Rascal, Chipmunk, Tinchy Stryder, Skepta, Ghetts... I was filming content for the Logan Sama show, and things kept growing from there. SB.TV got more and more hits, and the more hits you get the more people want to invest in you. I got the YouTube partnership first up, and I've started working with other companies, including Virgin Unite.

I put loads of energy into getting SB.TV off the ground – I was totally hands-on. But I did that because I knew that this wasn't something I was doing as a one-off, I wanted to keep doing it – keep shooting artists, keep getting those videos out there.

Even now, with a full team around me, there's ALWAYS something new that gets me going. I get thousands of emails with new tunes in, and every now and then there's something that just jumps out, and the moment you hear that is what drives you.

Media coverage and partnerships helped me to make SB.TV a full-time thing: I could quit my Topman job and eventually get a bunch of people working for me. But it's being totally fired up about what I do, Every Day of the Week, Every Hour of the Day that meant the launch of SB.TV was just the start of a much, much bigger journey.

And I want that to be the same for you – I want you to be able to do whatever it is you love doing and make it a success. So let's get on to YOUR story...

THINGS TO THINK ABOUT

Before you launch your idea, you need to do a final cross-check to make sure everything's in place. Think of your idea or your brand like your own private jet, and you're the one who's got to make sure all the doors are bolted so nothing goes wrong. Obviously there are some things you can't plan for, but you do need to do everything you can to make sure the worst doesn't happen.

Also, remember that the launch isn't the endgame. Imagine you're a rapper/singer and you're about to release your first single. You want to have a long career, so it can't be all about that first tune. Sure, you need to give it everything, but you also need to keep your eye on the bigger prize, which is a lifetime doing what you love.

Now's the time to make sure the groundwork's done so you don't fall at the first hurdle.

Make sure your social media's all on message

If you are launching a product or you're doing a gig, what's gonna happen when people visit your Facebook page? Does it have the same message your website does? Are they all up-to-date? Have you got someone else to check there are no spelling mistakes or pixelated logos? All this stuff is really important, and easy to forget.

Because SB.TV is an online brand, we have to make sure all our sites say the things we need them to – they all need to talk to our audience in the same way. So if someone goes to our Instagram feed, I want to make sure they get the same vibe about SB.TV as they would if they followed me on Keek or went to our Twitter feed. Basically all our branding has to be sick, slick and consistent, so people can see we're running a proper, on-it company. This means that more of them will come back again and again, which is what we need.

Be ready to keep up with demand

You also need to make sure you're ready in case the demand for your idea is higher than you'd expected. For SB.TV, that means having a 'queue' of videos ready, so we can meet the demands of our audience and always have another sick video on the way. So I have a schedule I keep to so I can make sure I have videos ready to post at the same times, every day.

If you're making a physical thing, like shoes or photo prints or whatever, you need to do the same thing. You need to have more lined up ready for when you sell out of all the stock you have. You need to imagine what you would do if someone wrote about your idea in a national magazine and then suddenly everyone wanted to buy, hear or see more of it. How would you deal with that? Could you meet that demand?

Make sure everyone's on the same page

As a visionary and entrepreneur, it's also your responsibility to make sure your team know what you expect of them when you launch. Everyone needs to be trusted to have their own set of tasks that they're going to do, because you'll make it harder on yourself if you try to do absolutely everything. You need to get your team to imagine problems they might encounter – and tell you how they would deal with them – so you can make sure they know what they're doing. All you're doing here, is getting yourself into the best state of readiness. Everyone needs to be on their job.

The other way to test you're really ready, is to record yourself. Use your phone or your laptop, and either make a sound recording or a video of you talking about your idea and explaining it really simply, in one sentence. Practise in the mirror a few times and then record and play it back. How do you sound? Do you believe what you're saying? Do you sound like you know what you're talking about? When you launch a brand you're going to get asked a million times to explain what it is you do, and why it's so special. So you need to get really good at doing that, and it's just a question of practice. So imagine you're being interviewed, or that a newspaper has asked you for a quote – a single sentence to explain your business or idea. Can you do that? Practise it until you can.

THE CHALLENGE

So, to get you ready for launching your idea, your start-up challenge in this level is to CROSS-CHECK. I need you to think about your idea from *every* possible angle – how are you gonna make money, what happens if your transport breaks down, all that stuff. OK? It's time to get this lot down. Get an A3 pad of paper and some marker pens, or a white board, and start emptying your brain onto it.

1. Make a list of the essential things to remember before launch – with your team or by yourself – and then re-order that list so the biggest tasks are at the top.

2. If you do have a team, get everyone to do a one-day jobswap, so that everybody's work is checked by someone else – it's much easier to spot mistakes in someone else's work than it is to spot them yourself.

3. However long your list is, make sure you tick off tasks as you do them. It might look full-on seeing it all written down, but the trick is to check off one big task plus a handful of small tasks every day. That'll make you feel like you're moving forward, rather than trying to tackle all the big ideas at once and not being able to get anywhere.

4. It's also a good idea to keep a pen and paper by your bed, because this stage of your day is when your brain is fizzing with ideas, and you don't want to be lying in the dark worrying about stuff – just get it down on paper. If you remember something that needs to be done, promise yourself that you'll do it tomorrow.

5. Once you've checked off everything on your list, do

something to celebrate: go out with your people, or if
you're in a team go out together and do something
that'll get you all in a hyped mood. Time spent getting
the detail down is tiring and can be pretty stressful so
you need to shake that off.

The most important thing at this stage is to be really sure that
you're ready to launch. The worst thing that can happen is if
you suddenly realised you weren't ready, and had to delay your
launch. But obviously it's much better to know that now, than
pulling out at the last minute and letting everyone down. I
want you to be honest, vigilant and true to yourself right now,
because you need this thing to be SLICK.

DECISION POINT

Time to head on and make your first choice – you rest
you rust!! So what are you thinking about doing?

Getting to 100% self-belief   **p 157**

Giving up your part-time job/college   **p 188**

Dealing with the money   **p 171**

STAGE 1: GETTING TO 100% SELF-BELIEF

I started hash-tagging #selfbelief on Twitter a while ago and it stuck: people respond to it, because it's the key to *everything*. You need it to follow your gut; you need it so you can be honest enough to look at the things you're not so good at; you need it to keep going through the hard times.

Where you are now with this idea of yours, it's like being a singer about to walk out on stage at a gig: you know you've put in the hours, you know you've got what it takes – but your heart's pounding like mad and all you can think about is the people sitting out there watching you.

That's why right now is when you've got to get your self-belief ramped up. This moment, before you put your vision out there, is when you've got to stop focusing on the negatives, and remember you've done everything you can to get this right and you're ready to share it with people. So what, not everyone's gonna like it, but loads of people will – and you need those people to see you giving them 100% of your self-belief, or they'll wonder why you're doubting yourself.

Pretend to be a hotshot PR agent

This isn't the time to be thinking, 'Oh shit I should have done this', or 'Maybe so-and-so was right about that'. You're where you want to be AT THIS STAGE, so here's what I want you to do:

1. For the next few minutes I want you to pretend you're
    not you. I want you to imagine you are your own PR,
    you're an agent representing YOU. You're never
    gonna hear a PR bad-mouthing their own client, so
    you can't either. Right now it's your job to put
    whatever you're doing in a good light, to present your
    idea as the one everyone wants, and everyone wishes
    they'd had first.

2. OK, so now you're a Hotshot Agent, I want you to
    remember the 60-second pitch we talked about in Level
    1. Only now, you're going to tighten this up even more.
    You're going to give your idea a strapline: write one
    sentence summing up the genius of your project.

3. Last of all, I want you to bang out four – and no more
    than four – selling points. These might be things like
    'It's never been done before, and there are xxx number
    of people who are into this, so there's definitely a
    market', or it might be 'Things like this do really well
    (give comparisons), and my idea is like this, but is
    cheaper/faster/better designed etc.'

Before you start to enjoy pretending to be someone else too
much, it's time to turn back into you – but keep that Agent
person in your head. Part of being confident sometimes
involves tapping into that energy and swagger that other
people have, and faking it til you make it. You've just been your
own PR rep, and from that you've got down the highlights of
your idea. Now you've got a strong, tight launch message right
there and your self-belief should be buzzing.

DECISION POINT

You've got your swagger on, now it's time to move on to the next stage. So what's your next move?

Alert the media p 166

Get connected p 185

STAGE 3: DO SOME GUERRILLA / VIRAL ADVERTISING

Guerrilla advertising is when people try to get attention for their company by doing stunts or mad things. For example, if you wanted to advertise a club night, you could get a load of people to dress up in morphsuits and run around your town with your logo or the venue/DJs written on their bodies. The idea is that you kind of ambush people and advertise to them in a non-mainstream way.

Keep your cool

The downside of this approach would be that you could come off as a bit try-hard/unprofessional – and that might not be an impression you want your brand to have. Also, if you only came across twenty people on the street, and they're all old and don't go clubbing anymore – your brand wouldn't be entering the minds of many, or at least not the right, people.

The other problem with guerrilla or viral advertising, is that you have to be completely original. That's really hard, because coming up with something no one has seen before can take ages unless you're a marketing genius. It's also hard to know which things are really going to take off on the internet.

I get sent 'comedy' videos all the time when people are trying to get my attention, but so often I get the feeling that although they may have been really funny to the people who made them, they're not funny to me. Humour is difficult – what you find funny, someone else might think is dumb. The way you have to think about it, is that there's nothing worse than a bad joke – if you've ever seen a comedian die on stage, you know how cringey it is. Also, the best kind of comedy is when it looks really effortless and spontaneous, unless you're a professional comedian it's really hard to do that.

Easy does it

For the first launch of your idea or business, I'm gonna be strict and advise you to keep it simple. Flyering, posters, social media and just getting out there and meeting people are the cheapest and best ways to find your audience, and see whether they're into what you're doing. Remember that you've only seen the internet memes or viral videos that actually worked – but there were millions that didn't and fell flat. All those bad ideas that *seemed like great ideas at the time* also cost money. And you need to keep your eye on your budget right now.

Now I'm gonna send you back to the Decision Point on **p 173** (if you came from Dealing with the Money) or **p 177** (if you came from Getting Public Buzz: Flyering and Street Advertising) so you can put your time and energy into ideas that'll definitely pay off...

STAGE 2: WHO'S DOING WHAT?

We've talked about making sure your team are all doing the job that fits with their skills before, but this is about making sure everyone is clear on what they're doing, and that they're doing it the way you need them to. You're heading into lift-off stage, so you've got to do your pre-flight checks.

Whatever level you're pursuing your idea at, whether it's a fun thing or a full-on 'this-is-my-life' thing, if you've got to this stage you'll have a team of people around you who've helped you develop it. You chose those people because they had skills that you were missing, and could help you do all the things you couldn't. These are the guys you trust to help you realise the vision, so it's important to make sure they're confident in what they're doing and that you're working together in a way that makes you all up your game.

One-to-one time

So, take time to check in with your team individually:

- Are they stoked about the launch? Get their energy up, and make sure they feel a part of it.
- Ask them to run through how their part in this is going – say you want to make sure they're feeling positive, and that they can ask you any questions if they're unsure about anything. ALWAYS make sure people feel relaxed enough around you to be able to ask questions, otherwise they'll hide problems that need to be out in the open.

- If you're concerned that they don't seem to have fully covered the ground, suggest drawing up a list of stuff to get back to you about by the end of the week, and arrange to check in again the following Monday to talk about it.

It's a big responsibility looking after a team of people – especially when they're working on an idea that's YOUR baby, it can be properly scary!! But you chose them for a reason, and they've got you this far so make sure they're still on the same page as you and pumped up to make the dream happen. If there are any issues, you need to get them sorted NOW. Once you're confident everyone is OK and things are running smoothly, you can get back to what you're supposed to be doing: leading the way.

DECISION POINT

Siiick! It's time to head on – you rest, you rust! So what's it going to be next? Choose a path.

Give away freebies to encourage interest   p 183

Throw a launch party to get media buzz   p 178

EUD OF LEUEL 4: OK, BUT I MIGHT NEED TO TRY AGAIN

Okay, so maybe you didn't get as many people to your launch party as you wanted. Maybe you did a dummy run of selling your service or product, and people weren't as into it as you expected. That's cool. What we need to look at now is why, so you can learn from this, improve and keep going. Having a vision is all about energy, it's about having the bravery to see something through and acknowledge any of your weaknesses, so you can work out what skills you need to hire in or learn for next time.

Pace yourself

You've also got to remember that this is still early days. We're at Level 4 but you might have read this book over a couple of months, which is no time *at all*. People act like I was some kind of overnight success but that's not true – I've been doing SB.TV for seven years! It just looks like it happened really quickly and smoothly because when things blow up, it looks like it's come from nowhere, when actually a lot of hard work has gone in to make it happen. So you need to have faith and surround yourself with positive people. Basically, don't get all messed up about it, stay focused and tomorrow you can improve.

The first step to getting over any disappointment is to celebrate what you did right. If one of your team was amazing at networking or selling your idea when you threw your party or did your dummy run, or if someone was great at marketing, you should praise them *now* for all the hard work they put in. It doesn't have to be anything major, just send them an email to say well done. At the beginning of any idea, no one is making much (or any) money, so all that's really motivating you is your enthusiasm and belief in your idea. If you've managed to survive on that energy up till now, you're doing an awesome job.

Could you do something different next time?

Then, obviously, there's gonna be the less fun thing of working out what you could have done better. Don't get messed up blaming people, just recognise the things that were under your control and that you could improve on. It's really important not to sweat the small stuff or the things which you didn't actually mess up. If the mistakes came from outside your team – whether they were people or services – don't worry about it. But you could decide not to work with them again, and set yourself the challenge of finding new contacts.

Whatever the mistakes were, first work out if you could have done anything about them (through planning or training) and then put them top of your list for next time. Every problem can be sorted out, you just need to focus, learn and move on. Because you need to be ready to GROW your idea in Level 5. Once you've had a think about what went wrong, maybe you want to give this level another go? If so, go back to the beginning of this level on **p 145**. Otherwise, I'll see you on **p 191** at Level 5...

STAGE 2: **ALERT THE MEDIA**

What's your angle?

When you're dealing with the media, you need to remember a couple of things. The first is that no matter how interesting your idea or product, journalists need an angle to sell your story to their editor. Freelance journalists who work for loads of different magazines and newspapers have to 'pitch' their ideas for articles to editors too, so there's kind of like a chain of command. You have to convince the journalist that you're interesting and current enough to write about, and they have to convince their editor that it's going to be an amazing article, that loads of people will want to read.

Put a hit list together

If you want to alert the media to get some free publicity for your idea, you need to start by making a hit list of papers, websites, blogs, magazines and journalists that you think are 'right' for your brand. Think about your target demographic and what kind of things they read.

- Do your potential customers read your local newspaper?
- Do they read a specialist magazine, like a music/food/ film mag?

Put yourself in your customer's shoes and think about what media they interact with. Then put that list in order of audience size, with the newspaper/website with the most readers at the top. You're going to have to work down that list, one at a time, so you can get the most publicity possible.

Fine-tune your press release

Have you already put a press release together? It's one of the options in Level 3 of *Self Belief: The Vision* – so you might have already done one. If you sent something out as a teaser, pre-launch, read it again and update it.

- Check that it's gonna speak to the people you're sending it to, the way you need it to.
- Imagine getting that press release and knowing nothing about you or your idea. Does it just tell you it's an exciting idea, or does it demonstrate that with examples and facts?
- Get someone else to read it and give you honest feedback.

Make a connection

Next, you need to find the email addresses or phone numbers for journalists who write for each of the media outlets on your list. Don't use generic addresses like 'news@' or 'info@', because these email accounts might not be checked regularly. You need to find out who writes about people who do things similar to your idea at that media outlet. Don't be afraid to look these people up on Twitter first – you can often find out loads of information about journalists on Twitter because it's their job to be out there, making contacts and finding out the most up-to-date information.

If you know more about who you're writing to, you can approach them in a way that's more likely to appeal to them.

You could also RT or chat to them on Twitter before you ask them to write about you or ask for their email or pitch your idea – that way it will feel more natural.

When you write to them, try to show the journalist what a good story it would make. If you've got an event coming up, tell them how many people are coming and why it will look good in photographs. Bring it alive, paint them a picture, so they get excited. If they're near the top of your hit list, you can also make it seem more exclusive by saying that no one else has written about you yet. Journalists love to get the scoop on new things, to be the first one to write about it.

Make sure you keep a list of who you've contacted/sent out a press release to. You don't want to keep hitting the same people up – it's a waste of your time and theirs. Stick your contacts in a spreadsheet and you can keep track of who you've covered.

Keep a record

My one last bit of advice would be to keep a press file. Seriously, I'm so mad at myself for not doing this and I wish I had a complete one now, because it's so good to look back and see how things have changed since I started my journey. And if you get someone to write about your idea, tweet me @selfbelievers! I wanna see those articles, articles are BIG!

DECISION POINT

Siiick! It's time to head on – you rest you rust! So what's it going to be next? Choose a path.

Give away freebies to encourage interest   p 183

Throw a launch party to get media buzz   p 178

END OF LEVEL 4: OH MY DAYS IT WAS BAD

Ok, so maybe you're feeling like some things went wrong; maybe you didn't make as much money as you thought. Maybe the contacts you needed didn't turn up to your party. That's okay. We just need to work out why before you can move on and try again.

You have to remember that the early stages of starting any business are the hardest of all – you're running around like mad, you don't know what you're doing, you don't have enough people in your team yet, if any. I get that, because when I started SB.TV it was just me. Then it was a few of my mates and we were all working from our bedrooms in our own houses. That's all SB.TV was – some kids with some computers, and some cheap cameras. But we still made it happen, and you can too.

Time to fix up

I'm a really positive person and I like to look on the bright side because it's what keeps me going. I don't like to get too bogged down. But sometimes you need to fix up and listen to that voice in your head. Not the one that's never on your side, not the really critical one. The other one – the one that's honest and who really knows why things go wrong.

I'm confident you can identify any mistakes you made. And you need to get into the mindframe of recognising that mistakes are just things that happen when things aren't quite lined up properly. Like when a beat is off in a song, and it sounds strange. Separate out your feelings and look at your mistakes cold, like it was just a thing that happened to someone else.

C'mon! The sky didn't suddenly go black, it's not the end of the world! It happens to everyone, and the thing that separates achievers from sheep is when you understand that mistakes aren't really a big deal. As long as nothing got hurt apart from your ego, it's cool.

Hold on to what you've achieved

The other thing to remember is that regardless of whether your idea worked, you still went through this process and did a load of work to try to make it happen. That in itself is an achievement because you've done something *real* – you've put your time and energy in to using the last few weeks or months in a different way.

I could have gone down a very different path when I was younger – and I definitely made some bad choices when I was a kid. But I decided to change my life and choose another way, and that's what you've done, too. So it hasn't worked out, so what? You really think you're only gonna have one good idea in your whole life? Or that you can't have another go and do it differently this time? COME ON. I know, and you know, that's not true.

Take a time out, go see your people, let off some steam, then go back to **p 145** and give Level 4 another go. Choose different options, do different tasks and you'll be ready for Level 5 (on **p 191**) in no time.

STAGE 1: DEALING WITH THE MONEY

Pretty much NO ONE likes having to think about money. We love what it can buy us, but it's a total nightmare to sort out things like budgets and accounts, and to stay on top of it all.

My mum was an accounts manager for YEARS before she got into singing properly, and she used to get me helping her out so I'd learn how to handle the money side of things a little bit. That doesn't mean I was good with money. I was a kid, right?!! But it did give me a pretty sound start for knowing how to check on what money was going in and what was going out.

Whatever you do in life, it is kind of a good idea to keep a track on where you're at with your money – whether this idea you're doing is something you sell or not. It's basic stuff really. You just need to write or type on a piece of A4 with a line down the middle. One half of the paper is what you're spending, the other is what money you've got coming in. So for me in the early days it would be the money I had coming in from Topman, and whatever I was spending it on – maybe tapes for filming or stuff kids usually spend their money on.

It seems boring and might feel like a waste of time, but if you've got an idea of what's going on with your money, you're in control, and being in control means you're able to get to where you want.

Get the price right

You'll have already looked at this if you're coming up to properly launching your idea, but if you're selling whatever you're doing to the public, you MUST make sure you're charging at the right level. When you start out, it's so important not to under- or over-sell yourself. You don't want to look cheap but you also don't want to look like you're ripping people off.

- Think about who you're selling to.
- Look at what other people are pricing their stuff at in the area you're selling.
- Know how much you spent on making your idea happen, and how that might factor into what you charge.

Later on, pricing can change – maybe you're doing well and you want to pitch something to people who might not have been able to afford what you did at the start, so you might do a cheaper range to target a new bunch of people. You see loads of clothes designers doing that.

Or maybe you find you have regular customers, but not loads and loads of them, so you need to slightly up the prices so it's worth your while, without scaring off your loyal support.

How are people gonna pay you?

As you're heading towards the launch, now's the time to really get on top of how you're going to process payment, if your idea is something that's going to bring you in money. There are loads of online sites that are set up to help you with this: Paypal, Google Checkout etc. You can always ask for cash payments but you'll have no record of it unless you're keeping a check on when it comes in. If you've set up a company, you'll have to sort out opening a bank account, and figure out about paying tax – unless you're lucky enough to have someone who can help you with this and sort it for you.

Remember: if you don't know how to do something,

someone else will. Parents, teachers, older brothers or sisters – they can all give you advice from their experience. Or go along to a bank and ask to speak to the manager who can tell you how to set up an account and what you'll need to do this.

Whether it's how to set up a bank account or fill out tax forms, hit up Google for tips and advice. Make sure it's an official site, like hmrc.gov.uk. Or you can always find courses to do in real life which teach you about all the things you need to know.

I kind of did things a bit back-to-front when it came to money – when things were really taking off, I got people in who knew how to sort out the money side of things. I didn't want to be bothered with all that when I started out. But these days I DO make sure I know what's happening with the financial side of it. If you don't understand it you make yourself really open to being ripped off. You wouldn't want someone to nab your idea, so make sure you don't let them mug you off when it comes to money.

DECISION POINT

Now you've got the money side sorted, what you gonna think about next?

Who's doing what?   p 162

Getting public buzz: flyering and street advertising   p 176

STAGE 3: SELL YOUR STUFF (SMALL SCALE)

Some people like to just go for the big-hit launch, where you throw everything at it and react flexibly to whatever feedback comes in. But not everyone's like that, and that's a good thing because if you're not the kind of person to be able to deal with all kinds of comments, it's good to be a bit more cautious.

One step at a time

So this is what's called a soft launch. You're putting out your idea to the public to buy into, but you're limiting what you're putting out there. If you're selling stuff – say maybe you make clothes – that might mean you put five products out on a site like Etsy or eBay and see what response you get. Or you could take them along to a local community event and see if you get any takers.

It totally depends what it is you're doing, but here are some different thoughts for how you might do a small-scale test-run:

- For things like clothes, pictures, jewellery, bags etc., Etsy and eBay are great cos you can set up your own online shop. List them at a price based on your research of what other products similar to yours are selling at.
- If you're in a band, or you're an artist, or a record label wanting to sell stuff, you might be better on a site like Bigcartel or Bandcamp.
- Local markets are good places to start out selling, particularly if your idea is a foodie thing. Go and ask

stallholders how they got set up, and whether there's a cost involved. The good thing about this is you can network with other sellers and get tips and advice, and also get known in the local community.

- Whatever your idea it can make sense to hook up with events or groups in your local community that are doing similar things to you. That way you can get a bit of support and feedback on how you're doing.

If people aren't biting, have you made sure that what you're selling looks as good as it could? Are your posters jumping off the wall? Is your online shop looking sick? Taking time to think about stuff like this will help things go smoothly later.

DECISION POINT

Hopefully that's given you the confidence to go out and sell your idea BIG TIME, or maybe it's given you some things to think about before you go all-out. So how did you get on?

Boom! Success	**p 181**
OK, but I might need to try again	**p 164**
Oh my days it was bad	**p 169**

STAGE 2: GETTING PUBLIC BUZZ: FLYERING AND STREET ADVERTISING

The one mistake that's easy to make is thinking that because your idea is great, word'll just get out. Truth is, you've gotta push this every step of the way. Don't expect success to be handed to you.

Back in Level 1 I sent you out on the streets to get feedback on your idea. The people walking down your high street, or hanging out in local shops or whatever, are the ones you need supporting you. Now you've got yourself up and running, don't put a wall between you. The internet's great for pushing stuff and getting word out, but you can't beat meeting potential customers face-to-face, and letting them know there's a real person behind this who wants to hear their opinions. Having this visibility is vital. People need to be given as many ways to find your idea as possible.

Hit the streets

There are different ways of doing this, depending what you think will work for your idea. These are just some thoughts, but have a proper think about it yourself because legwork like this can really pay off.

- Get together everyone who's been working on your idea and hit the streets with flyers. Don't hassle people, or beg them to buy into your idea – be friendly, give them a big smile and politely ask if they'd like to hear more.

- Postering is an old-school way of promoting, but that doesn't mean it doesn't work. Don't just slap a poster on a board with loads of others that probably look identical. Spend time on making it look good (remember that SIMPLICITY is best, always) and thinking about where you'll place it.
- If you've teamed up with a company or a brand, putting their logos on any flyers or posters might persuade them to help pay for them — you scratch their back...

The best thing about talking to people or handing out flyers, is that it makes it all REAL. Sending an email can be cool as you wait for the responses, but you get a more immediate buzz doing this. Get out there, tweet me @selfbelievers and let me know how you get on.

DECISION POINT

That's some tough work you've put in there. What do you want to do next? Pick a path below and let's go to the next stage.

Sell your stuff (small scale)   **p 174**

Do some guerrilla/viral advertising   **p 160**

STAGE 3: THROW A LAUNCH PARTY TO GET MEDIA BUZZ

Launch nights are fun, but you've got to think of them in a seriously practical way. It's not a party for your mates. It's not about getting wasted or having the best time. This is about your big idea becoming REAL. And you need to think carefully about what you're going to do, where you're going to have your launch, and who you're gonna invite.

If you keep going with your idea and make it into a long-term project or business, you'll probably have parties for other reasons down the line. You've got to think about what the purpose of your party is when you throw it, otherwise you could end up wasting a great opportunity.

This is your launch. Unless you're really lucky or you've got amazing connections, at this stage you're not going to be really well-known, so your launch is about getting in people who will be good at spreading the word, influencers in your industry and beyond. Write a list of groups of people you need to hit with your invite:

- Journalists/tweeters/bloggers – people who are going to cover the event for you and get the message out that what you're launching is officially off the ground.
- Anyone with power in your industry – you want these people to know about you, so invite them along. This isn't about proving you're competition; it's about showing respect. You want them onside.
- Mentors – invite along anyone who's invested in you;

people who've given you the time of day when they could have told you to get lost, who gave you good advice when you needed it.

- The public – these are your ultimate audience, so don't shut them out of a launch. You can't have your launch open to everyone cos it could go mental, but tweet about your event and say the first 20 people to reply can come. (If you need to put an age minimum on it make sure you put it clearly.)

Further down the line you and your team can relax a bit more at parties like this, but for the launch you're all gonna need to work it hard, and make sure you all have jobs to do that play to your strength, and get all the things you need covered.

1. Someone on the door – you don't want randoms turning up.
2. Someone checking people are OK for drinks.
3. Networkers – get people who are totally at ease with chatting to strangers and get them to work the people at the launch. Don't ram home whatever it is you're selling. If it comes up in conversation, great, but just being friendly, polite and professional is gonna be a good thing for the business.

Open the doors, and let's make this thing happen.

DECISION POINT

WOW. You did it. YOU DID IT! That's gotta feel good.
We're getting to the end of Level 4, so let's look at how
you're feeling about your launch. How'd it go?

Boom! Success   p 181

OK, but I might need to try again   p 164

Oh my days it was bad   p 169

EПD OF LEUEL 4: **BOOM! SUCCESS**

If you picked this path then your small-scale selling must've made you some cash, or your party was a success. Either way, you have a lot to feel really happy about right now. Because you've done it, man – you've had the confidence and the vision to stick with an idea of your own. And you've seen it through the first really tough stage, which is amazing. Some people give up early, or they get too scared to try out something new. You could have done that, but you didn't, so you should feel really proud.

This is all on you

Your *own brain made that money/pulled off that launch*, it *came from you*. You're gonna need to remember this feeling as we move on through to the next stages, because I want to push you to achieve more, and keep going. I think it's a good idea to celebrate this stage in your idea, and maybe use a small portion of that cash to buy something you can either wear every day, or put up in your bedroom. So every time you look at it, you remember this feeling.

If you threw a party, then I'm guessing some cool people came and that their feedback was good for your idea. This is really exciting too, because when you throw a party like that you're getting the kind of input you need – input from strangers or new acquaintances. To convert them, and get them into what you're doing, is such a big deal. There's nothing like creating a buzz and then getting to share that with people.

Make some memories

A good way for you to mark your achievement might be to make a wall of photos from that night, and all the things people said. Get 'em down on paper, put them up in your office or bedroom, so you can be reminded of everything you've done. And make sure you follow up on all the contacts you made – email everyone personally to thank them for coming, get a conversation going, so you can bring those people with you on your journey.

Once you've done either of those things, hit me up on Twitter @selfbelievers and tell me about it. I want to hear your stories. Even if you're stoked at how this level went, you might want to go back and take some other paths – get more ideas, and do some more tasks. Go back to the beginning on **p 145** and get as much as you can out of this level. Because soon it'll be time for Level 5 on **p 191**, where we're gonna GROW your vision, and take it to the next level. See you then!

STAGE 3: GIVE AWAY FREEBIES TO ENCOURAGE INTEREST

You like getting those freebies at stations, when they're handing out juice drinks or something, or when you get free samples in magazines, or free tickets to gigs, but has this actually made you go and buy what they're handing out free later on?

I'm not saying it's never a good idea to give things away for free, but there has to be a definite upside for you. I filmed free videos for friends when I started out, but I knew they were talented and that people would be into what they were doing, so it would be good for SB.TV's credibility and would bring traffic to the site.

At this stage, if you're giving away free stuff hoping people will be interested enough to find out more about what you're doing – rather than knowing there's a direct benefit – you're basically giving away money.

If you've been launching your own band, do you really want to hand out free tickets for your very first proper gig? Hopefully you'll get a great turnout but what if there are less people than you'd hoped and you make a loss cos you gave away freebies in the hope it would bring in more people?

Wait 'til you've got the cash to be flash

Apart from the fact that giving away something for nothing is bad business when you're in the early days of making your idea work, it kind of looks a bit desperate. When mega brands like Red Bull or Coca-Cola do giveaways, it's cos they can afford to do it and it looks good, being a big brand and being generous.

When you're someone no one's heard of and you're handing out stuff you've done for free, it screams I WANT YOU TO LIKE THIS!!

You're worth more than that and you know it. So hold your nerve, keep faith that you'll get the response you want, even if it's not at this very second. OK, now you've got that out of your head, let's get back to the Decision Point on **p 163** (if you came from Who's Doing What?) or **p 168** (if you came from Alert the Media) and take an option that's gonna help you progress.

STAGE 2: **GET CONNECTED**

You might not know this, but in most towns or cities, every week of the year, people get up at 6 a.m. to have breakfast and network. There are loads of different organisations that do this – Google 'business networking' and you'll find one in your area.

I know this might sound boring, and I'm not joking, but you might have to get up at like, 5 a.m. Anyone who knows me knows I'm not a morning person, but it's important to get your ass out of bed if it will help you get where you want to. There are people in those meeting rooms who could be incredibly useful to you. I don't think you should rule out *anything* in the early stages of your idea – and *Self Belief: The Vision* is all about challenging yourself – so this week I want you to go to a networking event.

Widen your contact base

A lot of networking organisations do things in the same way. What they do is invite one person from each industry and then ask them to find customers for the other, different businesses in that room. So if you were in the construction industry, you would be the only builder in your business network. If anyone else in the network came across someone who needed a builder, that business would automatically get referred to you.

Obviously the idea is that you're able to find potential customers not just from your own circle of contacts, but from the contacts of *all* the other business people in your network. So you widen your customer base really quickly.

HOWEVER the other angle I want you to think about here,

is that if you're young, you're going to be a bit of a novelty to these business people. People in business networks love to see a young person doing their own thing and having the confidence to make it happen. They're impressed by young people who are doing stuff to get ahead because they think all young people are just playing video games or lying in bed until midday. If they see you at their networking meeting, talking about your idea, most of them will want to help you.

Be prepared

A lot of business networks will ask you to stand up and talk about your idea – maybe even give a short presentation. So it's worth thinking about the following...

- You'll need to prepare and make sure you have a load of business cards, or maybe flyers, so you can leave your information with everyone in the room.
- Make the presentation short and snappy. (You could use the plan you made in Level 2 as a guide for what to include about your idea and how it works.)
- Think about what you can show them. If you have a video or presentation then that means you won't feel like all the eyes in the room are on you.

Basically you just need to tell your story and make it clear what you want from them – whether it's getting the word out, looking for investment or advice. There may be a possible mentor in that room, or a lawyer who's happy to give you some free advice because you're just starting out.

The other thing to remember is that you can usually go to one of these events for free, especially if you work the whole 'I'm just a young person, doing their best' angle. You could even be really cheeky and say that you need to come for your college coursework – I think it's okay to do this kind of thing when you get started. So it really shouldn't cost you anything to go.

Just make sure you swap business cards with everyone in that room, because you never know, the guy/woman with the sandwich business might be really amazing at business plans or know a really sick web designer. And you won't get all this useful information if you don't ask questions and talk to people.

DECISION POINT

That's some tough work you've put in there. What do you want to do next? Pick a path below and let's go to the next stage.

Sell your stuff (small scale)   p 174

Do some guerilla/viral advertising   p 160

STAGE 1: GIVING UP YOUR PART-TIME JOB / COLLEGE

If you've come from Level 3, you'll know that I SERIOUSLY believe you've got to figure out what the right path for you is when it comes to going to college or uni, or getting work experience.

You've now hit a stage where you're launching your idea OUT THERE; it's probably taking up a lot of your time and energy, and you're getting a buzz out of that adrenalin kick. It's one of those roller-coaster moments where your stomach's churning but you're not sure if it's cos you're freaked out or you're hyped up.

This is all probably making you think that it is time to quit your studies, or jack in that part-time job you've taken on to pay the bills; that it's time to throw everything at your idea to make it happen.

OK, let's hit PAUSE.

Time out

I'm stoked for you. Your confidence is up, you're fired up and ready to Do This Thing. But what you've got to do now is think of the bigger picture. Making your dreams happen isn't a 100m sprint. You've got a lot of stages to get through, and you need all the time and energy you've got to make this real.

So here's what you need to think about:

1. Have I got the passion to make this what I do every single day? Remember Level 2 when I asked you to

think about whether this is your calling or more of a fun sideline? Well, your idea might feel like it means Everything when you start out, but now you're at a stage where you're having to nail stuff down, maybe you're starting to question it. Be straight with yourself.

2. How am I going to pay my way if I quit college/my job? Don't say your parents!! It's great if you've got family to support you, but go back to Level 2 and think about how much you cost again. How much will it cost to keep yourself running WITHOUT trying to get your idea off the ground. Now factor in the costs involved in producing and launching your idea, and really make sure the finances stack up.

Being real about this stuff doesn't mean not having self-belief, or not being 100% behind what you're doing. It means knowing what is going to be a realistic strategy, and not blowing your chances of making it happen the way you want it to because you've got ahead of yourself.

Now we've had a time-out and put your head back on straight, let's go back to the Decision Point on **p156** and get back on track.

GOING
LARGE

Level 5

FOREWORD

There are many people who fantasise about their dreams coming true, but few that will actually go and make them their everyday reality: it takes a whole heap of dedication, confidence, passion, hard work and a great idea stemming from a great mind. Jamal has, and is, all of those things.

From day one Jamal has been fearless; a genuine independent young man with a mind swimming with ideas the world had to – and is now getting to – see. It's been a pleasure, not just to watch Jamal's journey but also to be a part of it and see the years of baby steps progress to what are now huge leaps of success.

I am so proud of him. I remember meeting Jamal and feeling his energy for what he does, as he spoke of his ideas with such poise and belief. The chance he gave me to be seen by audiences that may have never discovered me without his broad love of music, is amazing.

He is a true example and ambassador of self-belief for our generation, teaching young people that anything is possible. It all begins with a great idea. I am a true supporter of that.

Congratulations Jamal!

Jessie J, 2013

GOING LARGE

INTRO

I n this level we're gonna deal with how to make your idea grow. Maybe you've found some people you like to work with but aren't sure how to make everyone stay on their job, or do the things they're meant to be doing. Or maybe you're at the stage where it's hard to keep on top of all the requests that are coming in, and you're finding it difficult to decide which project to work on and which to turn down.

People are starting to come to *you*, and you're in demand. I love it when that happens because you get such a buzz from the energy that's floating about. You're rushing around to do all these different things and you barely have time to eat because people want what you're doing. You should always look at these times positively. If you're juggling a hundred different things, don't forget that you made those hundred things happen. Because you worked hard, and did your job well, and impressed people. I love looking around SB.TV and feeling like that.

Level 5 is about 'Going Large'. You've got your main idea down, you're getting great feedback and things are all on track. But this isn't the end of your vision: you've got bigger dreams. This level teaches you ways of making them happen. You might be working with a team of people by this stage – maybe you're working with people who were originally your friends, and that's an incredible thing, to be able to share your vision with people who've known you for a long time. But managing people can be hard, so we'll take a look at some ways of getting round any issues with that too in this level.

What you waiting for? Let's get this started.

MY STORY

Before my mum did *The X Factor*, she worked in the accounts department for a few media companies. So from an early age I remember being around her when she was working. Sometimes she'd take me into work with her or bring work home. She asked me to help her and it was bare numbers – I had to go through all these papers with one of those funny rubber thumb-thimble things. I'd always wondered what those were for.

I was proper young, but I'm glad she trusted me to help her sort out orders – even though we were dealing with some pretty important things, like the payroll for the company. I could have caused chaos. But working on accounts with her helped me understand how important numbers can be, and how you need to keep on top of everything if you want to go places in life. She was always really inspirational to me, because at a young age she stressed the importance of getting it right, and not messing it up.

When I started to put the team together for SB.TV, a lot of what my mum had taught me stayed in my mind. She worked so hard to make a career for herself after doing *The X Factor* and did loads of amazing things that I knew she wouldn't have been able to do if she hadn't been totally committed. It helped me to see that working in the media isn't always glamorous and that the most important thing is to work really hard and stay positive.

Learning from my mistakes

There was no point me crying like a baby about anything that went wrong, I had to look hard at myself and understand when mistakes were my fault or just bad luck. You have to keep moving and be an ambassador for your business. Whatever your idea is, you are that idea. You have to make people believe in you first if you want them to back your idea.

I wanted to work with people who got me, and understood what I was trying to do with SB.TV. So I had to find people who would work as hard as I do, but it was also really important that some of them filled the gaps in my skills – they had to be amazing at the things I was less interested in or less good at. We also needed to be really tight, so if we got any criticism we could stand together and be strong. Your team are your armour, and you all have to have each other's back if someone tries to take you down or when things go wrong. I love that I've been able to find those people, so SB.TV could keep reaching higher.

THINGS TO THINK ABOUT

Some people don't want to hear criticism and I was once in that mind frame. I didn't want to listen to what anyone was saying about what I was doing.

In the beginning, I would get a few idiots dissing what I was doing on YouTube – like you would with anything, I suppose. People would say small things about my videos like I should turn the beat down and I'd be like, 'Nah, man, you need to hear it' – I was just blind to it. But then it got to the stage where I realised I needed to listen to what people were saying, and take it on board. One thing that helped was that I was used to seeing that kind of thing, because I'd been on social networks for such a long time. I'd seen people having beef, it wasn't new to me.

I'm not gonna lie though, at first I used to get wound up and I would cuss them back. Now I know it's not worth it and I stay calm because I don't want to lose focus on what I'm doing. I also realised telling people to shut up on the Internet was no way to talk to a potential customer. My mum used to ask me why I was wasting time cussing out anyone who'd been chatting rubbish about what I was doing and she was right.

The difficult thing is that some people who criticise you will have a valid point, and if you want your idea to keep evolving and getting better you'll have to take on board what they are saying. And that's hard, knowing who to listen to.

When to listen to criticism

I always use the benchmark that if someone only has negative stuff to say, and all they're doing is dissing, then I can't use what they're saying in any kind of constructive way. But if people give a negative comment as well as a positive, I'll listen.

The other time I'll listen to them is if they give a reason for why they don't like something. So if someone said they thought the effects we'd put on a video distracted from the song or performance, I'd want to check that. These are two good questions:

1. Is this person only saying negative things, are they just hating?
2. Have they given a reason for why they don't like what you're doing?

If you use these criteria it'll be easier to deal with feedback, because you'll be able to ignore people who are just being ignorant or taking out their own unhappiness on you. Then you can just filter them out and be blind to haters or people who are just being negative for something to do. So if someone says, 'That video is rubbish' but they don't say *why*, I won't listen to it. But if they say, 'This video is crap because of *this,* but maybe you could do *this* to fix it' – I'll listen. You still have to be careful, because some people get into the trap of trying to please everyone. And if you try to do that, you just dilute your vision, and it becomes weak. Don't try to do whatever people say, because you'll be bland.

It's a tricky balance, because time is the one thing that gets more precious the more successful you become. But if you're able to separate out your emotions and deal with criticism in a calm, factual, organised way, it can actually help you get better. So that's what we're going to do now.

THE CHALLENGE

Step 1

OK, so the first thing you need to do is get two of the biggest pieces of paper you can find – A1 size, the back of a roll of leftover wallpaper, or a massive whiteboard – as long as they're huge, because you're gonna put them on the wall. Criticism hurts people when they let it cook inside of them, because it just rumbles around eating away at you. We're gonna put it outside of yourself, so you can feel in control and stay focused. It'll also help if you can do this exercise with someone else – so either do this task with the rest of your team, or pick one person whose opinion you trust. Don't just pick someone who always agrees with you though. You need to be objective and honest about this.

Step 2

Set a timer. This has to be a timed task, to make you work quicker and smarter. Give yourself roughly forty-five minutes. On the first piece of paper, spend ten minutes writing down all the negative feedback you've been given. Don't write down nonsense from the haters, use the criteria I've given you to decide what to write down.

- Do they also give a positive?
- Do they give a reason?

If what they've said falls into either of those criteria you've got to get it down. It doesn't matter if this info has come to you on

Twitter, Facebook, in the comments or in person. Then spend another ten minutes putting all the nice stuff on the other piece of paper. Again, not just, 'Hey, Jamal, you're amazing!' – cos although that's always good to hear, ultimately it's not helpful. You need to work out WHY your ideas or people are amazing, so you can then do more of that thing, or give that person more responsibility.

Step 3

Now spend ten minutes going over both pieces of paper. You need to try and work out if any of these points are valid, so put a score from one to ten next to each one – one being 'This criticism has no value' (I don't agree with it at all, it has no basis in fact) and ten being 'This is right on the money' (this person has a point we should try to tackle). If any of the negative or positive feedback is beyond your control, or affected by outside forces, like luck, you can ignore them. You only want to focus on criticism that makes sense, and that you can actually do something about.

Step 4

Take a look at the marks you've given those criticisms. Which ones do you and your team strongly agree with? Whose responsibility are these things? You have twenty minutes to decide which feedback you're going to do something about in the next week, and who's going to do it. Make a date NOW to review this stuff next week. No one is allowed to miss this meeting.

That's some tough, honest thinking you've done, but you'll thank yourself for it later – promise! To put a bit of energy back in the room, spend five minutes listening to a track you all like. Turn it up, go crazy and skank out. You should always end meetings on a high.

DECISION POINT

Now it's time to make a choice. Depending on how you're feeling, and where you're at with your idea, do you want to:

Make your team bigger   p 203

Deal with negative press   p 212

Scale up your idea   p 220

STAGE 1: MAKE YOUR TEAM BIGGER

If you're still the only one working on your idea, it's time to find allies. Or maybe you already have a team, but need to find more people to make this thing happen. Either way, this path is about how to go about hiring, so you find *the right people* to work with.

When I'm hiring, I want to find people who are as good as me, but at the stuff I'm rubbish at. I'm good at creative things, so I find people who are good at other areas of the business that I can't or don't have to do. So I might look for the Jamal Edwards of Accounts, or the Jamal Edwards of Contracts, or the Jamal Edwards of Fashion: people as hard-working as me, and with the same attitude, but skilled in the areas I'm not good at. If I just hired more people like me, we'd have a team of people who are great at making videos, creating strands, finding talent, but nobody would get paid at the end of the month because none of us would know how to use bookkeeping software.

As long as everyone in my team has the same mindset as me and they believe in my vision for SB.TV, it works. I like and work well with people who are really driven and have loads of energy, so it would be stupid for me to hire people who only do their thing in a half-hearted way.

Where do I find the right people?

As we expanded, I found my team in lots of different ways. Mainly, they were people I knew on social networks – friends of friends, family connections. I never used websites to hire anyone because I wanted to know the people I worked with. I wanted a proper word-of-mouth idea of who they were, and whether they'd be right for us, and if they were any good at what they did. I also like working with friends because it's nice to bring people up with you, so they get to be part of what you're doing, part of your story.

But if you don't know many people who are into what you're doing, you'll need to use other methods. Here are some starting points...

- To start with, you need to make sure you know what kind of job they're going to have to do, so make a list of the tasks you'll expect them to be on top of.
- Then think in a more vague way, about the kind of people you want for this. Think about characteristics, like do they need to be outgoing or have loads of initiative.
- If you already have a team, you need to think about what kind of person would fit in with them.
  - Do you need someone really positive with loads of energy to give your team a boost?
  - Do you need someone calm because everyone in your team is always kicking off?
  - Remember that a good team or office is about having a balance of people, as well as a balance of skills.

Advertising for people can be expensive if you decide to use an agency. So use things that are free first – like Twitter, Facebook and a mailing list if you have one. Make it clear to people how you want them to apply, too.

If you want to spend time reading through loads of CVs – bearing in mind that a lot of CVs sound the same, and people don't always offer proof of what they say they're good at – do that. But if you need someone outgoing, it might be better to ask them to make a video and upload it to YouTube.

You can also ask people to complete a task. With SB.TV, I could ask people to come up with three new format ideas for our Christmas schedule, to see if they're creative enough to work for us. Setting a task is also good because only the people who really want to do that job will bother to apply. And if the ideas they submit are not up to your standards, you can weed them out straight away.

Crunch time

When you have a shortlist, it's time to interview. A lot of people don't realise that interviewing people is a skill, because you've only got a short amount of time to try to get an accurate picture of what that person is *really* like. You need to find out quickly who they are.

A good rule for interviews is the 80/20 rule, which is that you should only spend 20 per cent of the interview doing the talking. The rest of the time it should be the person you're interviewing talking, convincing you they're right for the job. Don't make the mistake of trying to get them to like you, or spend the whole time telling them how great it is to work with you or how your organisation works. If they've done their research they should know all that stuff already.

You also need to ask questions that get them to justify themselves.

- If they say on their CV that they're good at working in a team, ask them for a specific example of a time when they had to do that.
- If they say they're good at troubleshooting, ask them the last time they solved a problem and how they did it.

Don't let them state, get them to demonstrate. This will get rid of anyone who's just put a load of stuff down on their application because they thought it was what you wanted to hear.

DECISION POINT

Once you've got a team together, it's time to take it to the next level. Do you want to know more about:

Managing your team	**p 214**
Finding sponsors/brand partners	**p 223**

STAGE 2: DO A SECOND MARKETING PUSH

When you first start marketing your idea to people, it's fresh, and everybody's like 'Oooh, new kid on the block' – the mainstream media rush to cover your business, especially if you're young, because a lot of the time they have this idea that all young people are up to no good. This can work for you first time around, because people think it's freaky and mad that you're being proactive and trying to build your own future. They'll write about you just because of that. Which is great, because – yesssss – free advertising.

After that initial buzz has worn off though, you probably need to have another push. People won't necessarily give you some of that sweet free advertising by writing newspaper articles about you, so you have to find a new way to get coverage. Remember that traditional advertising is really expensive, so the more you can do to get journalists interested, the better. Word of mouth is the best advertisement of all, but the only way to get that is to raise your game and do what you do, better. Hopefully you're working on that already.

Think like a journo

So for your second marketing push you need to get inside the mind of a journalist. Think about how they choose who and what to write about. Journalists have to pitch their articles to an editor – they have to get their editor excited. They do this by covering things that either haven't been written about before, or by writing about an old thing in a new way. You need to remember that when you're sending press releases or keeping your media contacts up-to-date.

If you've already done one angle to death, then you'll need a new one. Are you doing something mad or crazy that no one else is doing? If you are, use that. If you're not, you need to brainstorm a new add-on service maybe, or think about doing a competition that will grab people's minds, or find some brand ambassadors who can get the word out.

Be clever about it – do a collaboration with someone who already has a following, but maybe their following doesn't know about your idea or company yet. The person you do the collaboration with will be pleased to have access to your audience, and you get access to theirs. It's like when we do the SB.TV strings sessions – we're reaching out to people who might not normally watch SB.TV. It's a whole new angle to what we're doing.

Spend some time thinking about how to switch it up so you have a new angle you can sell to the media. Think about weird people for you to collaborate with which a wider audience would find really surprising. Collaborations take you down whole new paths and bring you into contact with new people which will energise your team and your business. Surprise yourself.

DECISION POINT

Now it's time to make a decision. Do you want to go on to:

Write your office/work rules   **p 227**

Avoid rules, keep it loose   **p 211**

END OF LEVEL 5: OK, BUT I MIGHT NEED TO TRY AGAIN

When SB.TV was growing I hired someone as my PA. Big up, she was a great person but she only stayed with us for a few months. There was just too much coming in, too much to organise and there were so many deals flying in – like Google deals, Puma deals and SB.TV deals. I was getting a hundred emails a day and sorting out meetings for me then was just mental. I didn't really know what she'd done before in terms of her work experience, I think she just wanted to try it, but SB.TV was just a bit much for her. I mean, it was mad then, because things were blowing up.

The point is that it was my fault, and it taught me a bit of a lesson. I realised then that I shouldn't hire people who hadn't had loads of experience.

This whole level has been about how you grow your business, and in a way, that's the hardest part. At the beginning, when no one is looking at you or tracking your progress, you're free to do what you want. You don't get as much criticism because nobody knows you exist. But you have to remember that to grow any idea you come up with on your own is such a massive deal, it is such an achievement. I hope you're proud of what you've done so far because most people barely even bother to try new things; they just get any old job and are too scared to branch out and trust their vision. That's not you.

Now is a good time to look at what's worked and what hasn't, because you only want to make each mistake one time. I've made mistakes, and after they've happened and everyone's calmed down I always end up having a laugh about them. You have to lighten the mood, so you can move on and keep going. There's nothing a phone call can't sort out, so I recommend that – face up to people, be cool with them. You know how quickly things blow over these days. Things blow up on Twitter one day and then there's nothing a week later. Mistakes get old fast.

Maybe it'll help you to have another go at this level? If so go to **p 191** to go back to the start and try some different options this time.

STAGE 3: AVOID RULES, KEEP IT LOOSE

People can mistake me sometimes because I'm so relaxed. For example, I'm always raving, and I'm always dancing, and happy around the office – so everyone else is happy in the office. I think if I was stern and strict in the office it wouldn't be as much fun. But sometimes I have to tone it down, because my team will look at me and think, 'Oh, Jamal's doing that, I can do that.' Like if I'm playing my music loud, someone else will play their music loud, and then it's a bit crazy.

What I'm saying is that everyone wants to be a cool boss, but sometimes you have to lay down the law. You know that thing people say about how little kids need boundaries? It's the same with adults, they need to know where they stand and what you expect from them. That doesn't mean your office has to be boring or that you can't have fun. But if we didn't have high standards at SB.TV, the quality would drop, our content would be bog. It would be too easy to mess about, and we wouldn't be on our jobs.

So when you think 'Rules', don't think of something made to control you, think about it like something there to help you get where you want to. Let's go back to the Decision Point on p 208 (if you came from Do a Second Marketing Push) or p 224 (if you came from Finding Sponsors/Brand Partners) and pick a different option this time.

STAGE 1: DEAL WITH NEGATIVE PRESS

How are people reacting?

We're at Level 5 now, so if you've been through Levels 1–4 you'll have already done loads of tasks and tried out loads of different things. You've also gone public in that your friends and family – and maybe now the world – know that you've got this vision. It's like in poker where you show your hand – people *know* you have ambition now, they *know* you want things for yourself. I love it when people are ambitious and driven, but some people get jealous and want to take you down. How's it been for you?

If you know my story you'll know that I've got into the occasional Internet beef with someone. It makes me laugh to think of it as beef though – cos these are people I've never even met; it's jokes! But if you believe in something, it's kind of inevitable that you'll take it personally if someone attacks your idea. And sometimes you just get into beefs because you're frustrated, because you're working so hard.

You can't win

I made the mistake of getting into a stupid beef on Twitter. I was tired and read something that was just so stupid and ignorant, I lashed out. I was in Croatia at the time working on a project, and I saw this tweet and just lost my mind. The person in question kind of has a profile so of course, it got out of hand really quickly and ended up with us both calling each other names and I even wrote stuff on photos of this person and posted them. And then of course the papers picked up on it, so it was in the *Daily Mail*, the *Star*, the *Mirror*, it was everywhere.

I deleted all the tweets because I just wanted to get away from it. But I couldn't, because nothing ever really dies on the Internet, even if you change your mind, see sense and take it down. The Internet has no erase button. So then the papers were trying to make me out to be a bully, and I was really angry, because I'm not like that at all. I was going to try and find the name of the journalist who wrote one of the pieces, so I could explain my side of the story. But Aaron, one of SB.TV's presenters, was like 'Jamal, don't get involved in this,' and he calmed me down. I was really glad he did, because it could have escalated even more.

All I'm saying is that you can't win with this stuff. When you start cussing people out – especially online – it goes from one to pointless in two seconds. What I should have done was to go and clear my head and then just stop looking at ignorant stuff on the Internet – because those people are always going to be there, and you have to forget about them.

Don't waste your time on ignorant people, chase your dreams, not the competition. OK? Let's go back to the Decision Point on **p 202** and take an option that's worth spending your energy on.

STAGE 2: MANAGING YOUR TEAM

The best kind of bosses can do all the jobs that everyone in their company can do, and the people who work for you should *know* that. You got them to work with you because they have skills where you don't, but you should still know what their role is and how to do it. All my team know that I can do their jobs, because I already did them in the early days of SB.TV. I don't say that to them as a threat, like 'Yo, I can do your job,' but all my team know I ran that channel pretty much all by myself for two or three years before I could afford to hire anyone. And I think that's a good way to manage. This also gives them confidence in a way, like, 'If Jamal can do it, so can I.' We've all got empathy for each other.

Your team should know you're not afraid to get your hands dirty, but also that you have high standards and that they can't pull the wool over your eyes. My staff know if they mess up, I could go in hard on them. They know it from my example, and the way I act around the office, and from what they've seen me do.

I think you should work with your friends at first if you can, but you have to make sure everyone knows what they're doing and that all your roles are distinct and clear. If someone does something wrong, regardless of how busy I am, I'll take over the task they were doing and finish it for them. And that makes them feel bad because they'll see me doing loads of meetings and doing everything I have to do, and *still* getting their job done as well. That makes them buck their ideas up.

Do they feel it?

When you hire someone to be part of something that was your vision, and that's always been your baby, you need to find people who share that love for what you do. I didn't want to hire people who thought it was, like, 'just a job'. And as time's gone on, I've tried to make them feel more part of it. I give them the smallest level of responsibility when they start with SB.TV and as time goes on, I keep pushing things in.

So with Ricky, I gave him the Facebook to run first, and then I gave him the Twitter, and then the Instagram – and then he handled booking-in videos, and then uploading videos, and now he handles making the videos public. After he's proved himself maybe he'll handle some of the projects, I'm not sure yet. It just slowly progresses like that. But if I gave him all those responsibilities straight away – and just go BOOM – he wouldn't feel like he had to work for anything. I want them to come to me and ask for more work, to say 'Aw, Jamal, come on, I've done the Twitter, gimme the Facebook,' and I'm like, 'OK, cool.' And then, in a while, they'll come to me and say, 'I've done the Twitter and Facebook, let me do something else,' and I'll let them start scheduling videos for me. You should let things progress like that, with them keeping stepping, stepping, stepping.

Keep your eye on the ball

When you have a vision for an idea and you're working with a team, there are a few things you really need to remember:

- **Don't forget why you're doing what you do – you have to not be distracted by money or success and get sidetracked.**
- **Be on your game, organised and streamlined, so you**

can fulfil people's expectations and run a business
that's slick.

- Surround yourself with people who get you – who
  want to be part of your story and grow with you. You
  all have to share the same aims and want the same
  things for your organisation.

To make that happen you have to lead by example. Not easy,
but you're at Level 5 man!! You can do it.

DECISION POINT

Hopefully you're hyped and ready to move on to the
next stage. What do you want to do next?

Make your work space look sick   **p 225**

Learn to share the workload   **p 232**

STAGE 2: PITCH FOR FUNDING AND GRANTS

Having a shopping list at the start of your business is a bad idea, because I think you should work with the gear you have, and work towards having the money to buy better. People often use 'not having' as a reason for 'not doing' which is stupid, because whatever you love or whatever field you want to work in, you have to practise it, and start as early as you can. You just have to do it.

But there may come a time when you have an opportunity to apply for a grant, or get the chance to pitch for some money from investors. And for this you need to know how to pitch.

I had to do a pitch when I applied to become an official YouTube partner. They make you explain why they should take you on and you have to show how you're gonna make it a success. Well, it took me five attempts. And I just kept going even though it didn't work out the first, second, third or fourth time. I failed *four times*. After I was successful, I even helped some of my competitors with their YouTube applications. I was only about seventeen when I got the partnership, so the best thing was getting to go home and tell my mum that I had my own money. I didn't need to ask her for money any more. It wasn't loads, but in the end it was enough for me to leave my job at Topman.

What's a pitch?

A pitch is a short, simple argument that identifies a problem and your solution to that problem. You have to make a case for your idea or product in a simple, persuasive, factual way. A good pitch should:

1. Identify a problem
2. Explain what happens if that problem is not fixed
3. Demonstrate (with facts) your solution
4. Show why you're the best possible person to solve that problem
5. Show how great it will be if your pitch is given their backing

The Google Chrome ad I did was kind of like a pitch, because it explained what I did and how I did it (I knew loads of MCs, I made emerging artists' videos when no one else was really making them online), how many hits I got (facts, the impact of my solution) and why it was so great for SB.TV (we just got bigger and bigger, I formed a company, got a label, made money, hired a team).

You should be able to think about your idea in this way.

- What gap in the market are you going to fill?
- Why is your idea the best one out there?
- Is what you do/make better quality than the competition?
- Is what you're offering cheaper? And if so, is that a good thing?

The best thing is to try to deliver a pitch in sixty seconds, out loud. This is called an 'Elevator Pitch' because it's designed to be said in the time it takes to go from the first to the tenth floor in a lift. So say I was at a major record label, and I saw Beyoncé in the lift, I'd want to be able to persuade her to do a video for SB.TV in sixty seconds. That is nothing, so I'd have to pitch it to her in a really sick, snappy way.

You need to be able to pitch your idea like this whether

you're looking for a grant, money from investors, or just want to persuade someone to work with you. You need it for networking when you're an ambassador for your vision. Work your pitch out now, so you can just say it naturally when you bump into Beyoncé ;)

DECISION POINT

Hopefully you're hyped and ready to move on to the next stage. What do you want to do next?

Make your work space look sick   **p 225**

Learn to share the workload   **p 232**

STAGE 1: **SCALE UP YOUR IDEA**

Scaling up means seeing if there are ways to maximise your idea and make it as powerful or lucrative as possible. You have to make sure you've worked out all the different ways you could apply your idea, and that you've maximised all the places where your product or service could work or be bought. You need to see if your idea could work internationally, and if it makes sense to be online, as well as in a shop. Always be ambitious, even if you need to wait until certain things are in place before you can expand. Know where you're going.

I have a tendency to be kind of impulsive, so I didn't spend very long thinking about how to expand SB.TV. I just did it one night. I got home and thought, I'm gonna start a load more channels and I did it without talking to anyone at SB.TV. I just set them all up, click click click cliiiiiick. I felt like if I told too many people about my plans, they might have given me reasons why we shouldn't do it. And I didn't want to think like that, I didn't want to hear anything negative or cautious.

But because I didn't talk to my team, it kind of went wrong. I hadn't really thought it through properly and that was a big mistake, because I had to redo all the channels again and then do another big marketing push to make sure people knew about them. Although having new channels was a good idea, I'd accidentally made it much harder for myself.

Plan before you make your move

If you want to expand your idea, you need to make sure it's planned properly. Because when you replicate an idea you have to make sure you're not diluting it or making it weak. So like if you're doing a blog about gigs in the UK, you might want to get someone from Manchester or Birmingham covering gigs in those areas, but they still need to have the same idea about what the blog should be like, and the same passion for music as you. Just like when you hire people, every single person in your company has to share your vision, and there have to be regular checks in place to make sure you're all working in the same way. That's why targets can be good, because you can measure success. You also need to make sure everyone is communicating regularly, so no one goes off and does something crazy that doesn't make sense for your idea.

Who else can you reach?

You can also just expand by selling what you do to a new and different set of people. In theory, we could start an SB.TV for people who are older, and create videos that appeal to them, because we already know how to structure our videos and produce them so they look sick. We've not done this, because we've decided to expand horizontally, making different channels that appeal to the same set of young people. We've also expanded by making videos for organisations who want to talk to young people in the right way, like charities or fashion brands. All we're doing is using our skills and selling them to a new set of people.

Spend some time now working out all the ways you could apply your skills to bring in a new audience, or more potential customers. If you play guitar, the obvious money-making avenues would be:

- Work as a session musician
- Make your own music
- Teach guitar playing in schools and colleges
- Offer private tuition

But you could ALSO run one-off workshops where people get to learn how to play their favourite track, or offer access to online tutorials for those people outside your area. You could get those tutorials sponsored by a famous guitar brand and make money from advertising. You could publish your own ebook on how to play. Or do lessons on Skype. Or write music beds for adverts or short films. Think about your idea in this way, to make sure you're not missing out on any opportunities.

DECISION POINT

And now it's time to make a choice. Do you want to go on to:

Pitch for funding and grants   **p 217**

Do a second marketing push   **p 207**

STAGE 2: FINDING SPONSORS / BRAND PARTNERS

Finding a good match

At SB.TV I still sign off on all the videos before they get uploaded. This may sound a bit control freaky but I have to make sure I'm in charge of our output and that the quality of SB.TV never drops. It's the same when you find brands or partners who want to work with you – you have to make sure their involvement doesn't interfere with what you're doing. Their brand should complement your brand. It should 'make sense' that your two companies work together. It's like if you saw someone cool who you respected advertising insurance. You end up thinking both the brand and the person are rubbish.

Knowing who to work with can be tricky, though, especially if some company is offering you a load of cash. I did a deal with one company, and I chose them because they were one of the first brands to holler at me. Obviously when I started getting hotter and hotter loads of people started hollering at me, but that company had been there since the beginning. So my loyalty – even when that first deal finished, and I could have got another deal with another brand – was still with them. They hollered at me when I wasn't really that hot, and saw something in me, so I did a deal with them.

Keep your eyes open

People who are on their job notice up-and-coming companies or people, and want to work with them. But you have to be careful that they're not into working with you for the wrong reasons, because there are snakes, who just want to get a piece of what you're doing. I had some companies who would offer me stuff for free – clothes, studios, whatever. But it isn't *really* free if down the line they're like, 'We've done all this work for you, for free, now we want something' – because that's when they ask for a share of your company. So you need to know that some of the people around you, especially when you start to make it, are in it for something. Don't think it's all flowers and roses. Everyone wants a pay cheque; they want a share.

I still own all of SB.TV, and although I was nearly foolish at one point, I've never thought about giving any of my company away since. I learned from that first time. You just need to be smart. If someone's asking you to sign something and you don't understand it, you have to get advice. If you can't afford a lawyer you should at the very least ask your parents or a tutor. Basically, don't take too much free stuff off anyone if they're not your family.

I'm not saying take the piss with your family, but don't think, 'Oh, this person is giving me stuff out of the kindness of their own heart,' because they're not. If you're young, there'll be companies or snakes who know that you don't have much money and are gonna be tempted by free stuff or free clothes. Just be smart and remember, there's no such thing as free in business.

DECISION POINT

Now it's time to make a decision. Do you want to go on to:

Write your office/work rules p 227

Avoid rules, keep it loose p 211

STAGE 3: MAKE YOUR WORK SPACE LOOK SICK

It took SB.TV years until we could afford to have our own office. In the early days we would get cheaper rent by doing a deal with another company – we'd offer them free advertising on our site, or promote them through our videos in return for a few desks in their office. So before you start signing up for a sick office in a really nice block, think about whether it's cheaper to get a few desks at someone else's office, in return for you working for them.

I know a guy who started a fashion brand and managed to get access to state-of-the-art screen-printing equipment by being based in one of those shops that sells logo T-shirts to football teams and cleaning companies. He could never have afforded that equipment himself, but he got access to it by working for the guy whose company it was (he worked in the shop, but also ran his business from a desk in the back). That's the kind of smart thinking you need to do.

Slick space costs £££

I really like where SB.TV are based now, because we're in Central London, but you have to know that wherever you are, offices cost bare money. So making them look sick maybe shouldn't be top of your list. I used to have meetings in Starbucks, so many meetings. I did them there when I was based at my mum's house, and when our offices weren't that slick. That's cool though, because if you don't have an office or your offices are a bit rough, then just don't invite people there.

Sometimes it's good to have a bit of mystique around where the magic happens – like you're working out of a secret bunker or something. So if your office isn't that glam, don't get messed up about it. Find another way.

The other thing is that it doesn't actually matter what equipment you're using, as long as you're producing good work. The best ideas can be written on a Post-it note, and the best people don't need to hide behind their gear. Basically, what you *do* is more important than what you do it *on*.

So I'm gonna send you back to the Decision Point on **p 216** (if you came from Managing Your Team) or **p 219** (if you came from Pitch for Funding and Grants) now, because I don't want you to be distracted by ideas about crazy expensive desks or computers. If you're thinking too much about appearances, you're missing the point, so let's go back and get you on track again.

STAGE 3: WRITE YOUR OFFICE / WORK RULES

What's right for you?

I usually come into the office at 10 a.m. and stay til 6 p.m. But sometimes I'm at my office until midnight, if that's what it takes to get something done. The great thing is that when you run your own company, you get to decide how you work. If you look back, people haven't always worked from 9 a.m. to 5 p.m., five days a week – if you get into the history of people's working lives, it's not always been like this. So if you run your own company or team, it's up to you to find the best way to work. Ask yourself some questions, like:

- Do you even need an office?
- Could you all just be based at home, and then do a twice-daily video call?

You need to really think about what's gonna benefit you, before you waste any money.

You also don't have to act like they do in offices on TV or the one your mum or dad works in. At SB.TV, we play loud music whenever we want, and I sit with everyone so they can talk to me if they need to. In some companies the boss will be in an office away from everyone else with the door closed. But that wouldn't have worked for us, because sometimes we have to make quick decisions. I can't be messing around in my own office like I'm better than everyone.

I've also got people who work for me that are older than

me. That was daunting, but I made it clear that I want everyone to be free – so you don't have to go through loads of people to get to me. I'm *there*. This also means I know what everyone is doing all the time, because I can see what they're doing.

I also think it's important that you treat your team when they do well – we go raving, or go to Nando's for lunch, stuff like that. But only if I'm sure they're listening to me, and they're doing things properly.

Forget the rules

So the last thing I want you to do in this level is to write a work manifesto. Make up your own rules for how you work, so you can get the most out of your team. Don't think about it in terms of what you're 'supposed' to have, do what makes sense for your team. It's mad that there are so many unique people in the world, but we all work in the same kind of offices in the same kind of way. So shake it up. You could...

- ban email
- do regular job swaps
- make all meetings last twenty minutes MAX

Basically, be free and work out the best way to be the most productive. Think BIG. Once you're done, tell everyone in your team and get them to sign up to working that way, so you're all in tune with one another.

DECISION POINT

We're nearing the end of Level 5 now. How are you feeling?

Boom! Success   **p 230**

OK, but I might need to try again   **p 209**

Oh my days it was bad   **p 235**

END OF LEVEL 5: **BOOM! SUCCESS**

I love it when people are buzzing about their lives, it's infectious. So if you're starting to be successful, you should definitely take time out now to celebrate. It's funny how it all happens, though, when it starts to really hit home that you're having an impact, that things are changing, and it's all because of something you started. I love that.

For me, it was when my family from Luton started to hear about what I was doing without me or my mum telling them, and it was mad. I mean, they don't have YouTube or whatever. And then they're seeing me in like *The Sunday Times* or on the front of *Q* magazine, and it had this headline 'Meet the New Simon Cowell' – stuff like that, it made me proud.

And then when my mum started congratulating me on my work, that was really good, because obviously my parents aren't from that world. My mum's friends were coming up to her and saying, 'Is that your son?' If I do a video with an amazing grime MC, my mum and dad won't really get it. Especially in the beginning, because they didn't watch stuff like SB.TV, like most parents they just watch the mainstream media. But all of a sudden I was in the mainstream, and they could see me on CNBC – a BUSINESS CHANNEL – being talked about as an entrepreneur. They were like 'RAAAAAAA!' – they could see that I was really doing something.

So what I think would be good now – maybe after you've gone out raving to celebrate – is to go home and actually tell your parents, your family, whoever's closest to you. Show them what you've achieved. Parents often complain that their kids don't tell them what they're doing so I guarantee they will want to know this. Don't assume that just because you're doing something that appeals mostly to young people they won't be interested. There's something about celebrating with your family that feels different, so don't miss out on that.

Now you've done Level 5, I'll look forward to seeing you on **p 237** at Level 6. But to get the most out of this level, why not go back to the start on **p 191** and choose different paths this time. There'll be different things to think about and different tasks. Go on, try this level again!

STAGE 3: LEARN TO SHARE THE WORKLOAD

When I first started making videos for SB.TV I remember spending hours trying to upload them to YouTube so that I could get the perfect conversion rate. Some people I knew couldn't be bothered to go that extra mile – they thought it was a waste of time. But even though it would take like an hour to save the file, and another two hours to upload a video, I did it. I would try uploading it two, three, four times until it was right. I just kept on doing it, for days, until I got it perfect. Then people would ask me how I'd done it, because they assumed I'd worked out a magic short cut. But I hadn't, I had just been willing to put the time in.

Give clear instructions

When you work with other people you have to teach them in your own image. They have to understand what you expect of them, and what your standards are, if you want things to run smoothly. So the first thing you need to know about delegation is Give Clear Instructions:

- Don't waffle, make it clear in words of one syllable what you expect someone to do.
- Give them a time limit, so they know there's a deadline.
- Make sure there are consequences if they don't do it on time.

Sometimes people wanted to work for me just so that they had the SB.TV name, they wanted to be associated with us. Which is a bit mental. But I've learned a lot about character now, so these days I think I can just feel it, if people are right. The way they speak – I can't explain it, I can just feel it.

I want people to work for me who just know the brand and are able to talk about it and express it in the way I do, so they're part of it. I need them to share the same vision. Because when you've got the team that shares the same vision, they'll run the world for you. When I'm off in America, Japan or wherever, I know my team at base are handling it as if I was still there.

You can't do it all yourself

You also have to remember that you can't do everything yourself. It's really hard when something is your baby, because you don't want to let it go, especially if you've worked really hard. But delegation is really important if you want your vision to keep on growing, and you have to trust people. If you can't trust your team to look after things for you, maybe you've hired the wrong people?

Also don't forget that if you have a mentor or you decide to appoint a board you can delegate UP. That can be really cool – if you have a team of people who want to give back or help out your business or charity because they're into what you're doing. That's gonna take the pressure off you, if you're running this thing, because there'll be people you can call about the big stuff, even if it's just to run something past them. You don't have to do it alone, all the time.

DECISION POINT

We're nearing the end of Level 5 now. How are you feeling?

Boom! Success   p 230

OK, but I might need to try again   p 209

Oh my days it was bad   p 235

END OF LEVEL 5: OH MY DAYS IT WAS BAD

OK, I get you. You've done a load of hard work, but you're flagging so you're not sure if you've got enough to give it the final push and get the support to make this idea go large.

The Google advert was one thing that really put SB.TV on the map. It was like, I could pretty much do what I wanted after that – film at whatever hours, film wherever whenever – I didn't get questioned about it any more. Before that my parents would always be asking me, like 'Where you going? What you doing?', all that. But when I got co-signed by the media they were cool. Now they say, 'You must be doing something right to get a Google ad that's all over the TV.' I mean, I think they were already behind what I was doing, but as time has gone along it's got easier for me to have freedom to do what I want.

If you feel down about what's happened as you've been going through this level, you have to fix up and have faith that it can only get better. When I was fifteen, if I'd had to imagine what my life was going to look like, I'd never have imagined it would end up like this. Not when I was arguing with my mum about going out to film people, no way. So you've got to trust me that sometimes it looks like everything's always gonna be dark, but you have to expect the unexpected! You have to believe.

I always daydream that one day I will have a big building, like Donald Trump's in Las Vegas. Each floor is gonna have its own area – one floor for music, one for comedy, one for fashion, one for business, culture and so on. And then my top floor would be my home. I love *Home Alone* and *Richie Rich*, and when I watched them as a kid I would dream about having my own home, with studios in there, so I could live in my workplace. I just wanna be on the top floor and go straight to work, without having to leave the building. And so I keep on working, because that's the dream. You have to stay focused.

Go back to **p191** and have another go at this level – try some other options this time. Or write down what it was you found hard, or what you struggled with and see if you can figure out why. Get people you trust to look at it with you. You'll get there, just don't call it quits now. Get your self-belief up, and go to the page opposite for the final level of *Self Belief: The Vision*.

KEEP IT
FRESH

Level 6

FOREWORD

There are a couple of things that Jamal and I have in common: one, we are both very ambitious and dream big; two, we both worked at Topman (true story!). But the similarities don't stop there. The main thing that struck me about Jamal is that, like myself, he is very honest about how he got where he is. That same honesty is what I offer whenever a young actor asks me, 'How can I be like you?'

This book has honesty as a part of its DNA, the truth about the hard work involved in realising your ambitions, your confidence and skill set. Most people find it a challenge to ask for advice and it takes even more dedication to take the time to read it in the pages of a book. This book is worth that investment of your time, it's worth you doing the exercises because it will force you to be honest with yourself. Go get it.

Idris Elba, 2013

KEEP IT FRESH

INTRO

Woooo! You've made it to the last level of *Self Belief: The Vision* – you've totally got what it takes to make it, and I can't wait to hear your stories. If you haven't already, tweet me @selfbelievers so I can see what you've been up to.

SB.TV has never really felt like a job or a chore to me, because I still get such a buzz from uploading our videos and seeing the reaction they get. When everyone's talking about something we've done, the energy is mad. I always liked that saying, 'If you choose a job you love, you'll never work a day in your life.' Because when you've turned the thing you *love*, into the thing you *do*, your job doesn't feel like work.

I hope you've had a taste of what that's like already, and you've been able to create something you feel proud of, that other people enjoy. But when you get to this point you do need to stop and take a look at where you're at: maybe you're spending too much time working, and not getting out and letting off steam; or maybe you've got a bit stale in your vision and need to freshen it up. That's why this level's all about getting that buzz back, and remembering why you did this in the first place – and looking at how you can keep on keeping on well into the future.

Level 6 shows you how to keep things interesting as your vision expands and those early days or hard times, are like a million years away. It's about stopping to look at your story so far but also thinking ahead, to see what the next stage in your vision's gonna look like. We're gonna do a lot of challenges in this level, because I want you to keep pushing yourself. You still have no idea just how much you're capable of.

MY STORY

Looking back

When my mum got through to the finals of *The X Factor*, it made me feel famous. I was getting on the bus and people were saying, 'Oh my God, it's Brenda off *X Factor*'s son!' – all of that. And now it's the other way round, because people are saying to her, 'Oh, Brenda, you must be so proud of your son.' It's so funny. But now the tables have turned, and she's like, 'Yeah, yeah, that's my son.' It never occurred to me that this would happen, and it would be switched around like that.

When people write about entrepreneurs they always make a big deal about how they learned how to make money at a really young age. I had a little bit of that, but I wasn't *careful* with money as a kid. I had a piggy bank, but it used to get broken every week so I could buy stupid stuff like Alien Pods, Tamagotchis, FA football stickers, Beyblades... But that's normal. Most kids are shit with money to start with.

I've had to learn that, or hire people who knew how to help me with it. Also, money's not the motivator for me. I'm not saying it's not nice to be able to treat people now I can. When I was a kid, I used to get money for my dad's Christmas present from my mum, and get money for my mum's present off my dad. I love that I can buy my mum an iPad for her birthday now; I like being able to buy people nice things.

Still building the vision

The main thing about success is that it stamped me as an official person in the mainstream media. If you're covered in the mainstream media it gives you validation and it shows other people from your background that they could do it too. I do want young people to look up to me and I hope, if they know my story, they'll think, 'Well if he can do that, I can too.'

Getting media coverage also opens doors. So if you're at the stage where your idea or company or business is starting to get mainstream interest, don't shun that straight off cos you're worried about credibility – though don't do anything that's not you. It's great when underground media covers you, but the mainstream can really open doors, and that'll help your vision grow.

I'm proud to be involved in doing stuff I wouldn't normally – like the Manchester International Festival – because it breaks me out into a new arena, it puts me on another level. I've come from West London, and I've met Richard Branson and worked with the most amazing artists – it's just mad. I know things like this could happen to you if you stick with what you're doing, and keep your focus.

THINGS TO THINK ABOUT

What you've achieved

So, the first thing I think we need to do is take time out to think back on what you've done. When you're mad busy with a new venture, you're in this crazy mindset because you're just running from one thing to the next without having a chance to look at the bigger picture. But it's really important to do that. Because if you sit back and feel proud, that pride and confidence will keep you going through any hard times that might be ahead.

Some things that happened to me might have looked like failures at the time, but they were kind of like stops along the journey. And some failures can even be funny further down the line. Like, I applied for an internship at MTV when I was younger, and they turned me down. I was really disappointed. But then, years later, they asked me to go down and do a talk to all their staff. I got one of my team to film it because it was a real moment. God, just a few years ago, they didn't want me!! And then they wanted me to come in and talk about my story. That's just a weird thing.

That made me want to document things a lot more, because so many things happened when SB.TV really started to take off, and I don't have a record of them, except in my head. That was one thing I worked out only recently – I need to keep more stuff, like photos and press clippings. I don't even have some of the fox videos I made! And they were the very start of SB.TV, they're part of my story. I didn't realise I needed to keep them but I should have.

Remembering your support

One of the first people I managed to meet in the media industry was Joe Godwin, who is Children's Director at the BBC. He managed to hook me up with someone else to give me work experience, but I still made a point of emailing Joe and anyone else along the chain who had helped me get that placement. And then when the work experience was over, I emailed them again to say thank you and tell them it went well. I also wanted them to keep me in mind for the future. Small things like that make a difference.

So I make sure that every time I do something big – whether it's something like being on the front cover of *Wired*, or *The Sunday Times* piece – I will always email these important people to let them know how I'm doing. I've emailed with Richard Branson a couple of times and Chad Hurley, the co-founder of YouTube, and also actor Idris Elba.

I also think it's nice to reconnect because from a selfish

point of view, it might actually help you. If someone believed in you right at the beginning, they will want to know if good things have happened since. Then they can show it to their friends and be like, 'Remember that kid, Jamal, look what he's doing now!' This could bring you into contact with a whole new set of people, who might be useful. You just never know. Following up is really, *really* important. Regardless of who these people are, they still gave you a chance.

THE CHALLENGE

Putting the past behind you

OK, now let's put that thinking time to use. I want you to look at what's gone wrong. I don't like to be negative but we've all made mistakes we can learn from, and if you can't work out what they are, you'll make them again. You need to promise yourself to deal with anything in your team that's not working. Remember that one of the signs of someone making it are when they've survived some hard times and have a few funny tales that they can laugh about with their team. You know, when you go, 'Oh. My. God. You remember that time when...?' If you've got a few of these, don't worry. You don't have to share them with the world, but you do need to be able to see the funny side. So do it.

- Sit down with the people who've helped you realise your idea, and share stories about things you've each done wrong, and LAUGH. This isn't about blame; it's about accepting that the road to success has loads of obstacles in the way – but you got round them together.
- Once you've done that, move on and look to the future.

Next, think about your numbers, whether it's how many hits your website is getting, how much of your product you're selling, how many people you've got coming to your event, or how many followers you have on Twitter.

- Set some goals, so you know where you're going, and review your progress every day.
- Put each person on your team in charge of something, so they all feel like they've got their own individual purpose, but also that you're all part of making this thing you've created bigger, stronger and better.

Now you need to work out who to thank. Be humble, this isn't about bragging about where you've got to.

- Write them a personal message whether it's a text or email. These are the people who invested in you – even if they only took ten minutes to answer an email from you way, way back in time. If you're in a competitive industry, then you already know how hard it is to make it and how mad it is. So that ten minutes they took out of their schedule to help you – maybe they didn't even know you – that was precious. Pull up that old email, and send them one back to say thanks.
- Let them know where you're at with your idea, and how things have gone, and what their support meant to you. It's not sucking ass – they will appreciate you remembering they were there for you, and seeing your success will make them feel good about supporting you.

This challenge has been all about thinking about how far you've come, being cool with your mistakes, and putting yourself in a good place to move on to the next step. If you take the time to do these small things now, it'll put you in a good headspace.

DECISION POINT

How're you doing? What is the main thing on your mind right now? We're about to head into the first stage of Level 6 so it's time to make a choice. There are three paths to choose from — which is it gonna be?

I want to make my idea slicker	p 250
I want a holiday	p 258
I feel like a sell-out	p 281

STAGE 1: I WANT TO MAKE MY IDEA SLICKER

When you first come up with an idea, you go through that early, crazy stage of daydreaming about it – 'Imagine if this happened... what if that happened.' I love that initial stage, because it's all about your dreams, you have no idea what's ahead and no reason to limit your goals.

If you feel like you've hit a wall and want to improve what you're doing or bring more people in contact with your idea, you need to get that feeling back. Because you have to be really open-minded about all new avenues you, your team and your idea could go down. That can be hard because once you've been in your game for a while, you know a bit more about how things work. And a little bit of knowledge is sometimes a bad thing, because once people have learned the rules of a particular game, they start to think they have to play by them all the time. When you started, there were no rules. And that's the kind of mindset you'll need, if you're looking to expand your vision. It's like when I asked you to Be Cheeky in Level 2. You're still allowed to do that.

When you brainstorm new ideas for your team, make sure you remember that there are no 'Buts'. So no one is allowed to shoot stuff down or think up reasons why something *can't* happen. Just get the ideas down and get excited about them. Here are some topics so you can keep it focused:

- **Upping your production values** – Is it time to invest in some new equipment or gear which will improve the 'finish' of your product or service? Only do this if you have enough money to, as I'm not a great believer in debt. But you may be in a better position to negotiate deals now your profile is higher.

- **Changing your online presence** – We've changed the SB.TV website loads of times because I didn't want things to get boring. I wanted to embrace all the new social networks, so we've picked up on things like Instagram and Keek as they've launched, and told our audience about them. Pick a new design that won't get old, i.e. a look that isn't too of-the-moment, especially if you won't be able to upgrade again for a while.

- **Market research** – This isn't something you should just do when you start a new business or start to research a new idea, like in Levels 1 and 2. Now you have a following or clients, you need to reach out and find out what they think, and what they want that you don't currently offer. See if one of your team can persuade some of your followers to take part in a survey, in return for a discount, or access to some special content or products.

- **Modernising** – It might be that your skills and training were really hot when you first launched your idea. But are they still? Any team has to evolve and embrace new ideas, because you need to stay ahead of the curve and lead, not follow.

- **Changing your product line** – Say you have a product which can only be consumed by people once (like, say, an iPod). How do manufacturers get you to buy more of such products? By adding functionality, making them smaller, more powerful? You need to rethink your 'product line' (even if you're a charity) regularly.

- **Limited runs and collaborations** – People love limited edition things, it's a way of adding value and making what you're doing seem more sought-after. If you're running a fashion brand, you could make a limited run of T-shirts with a respected illustrator or artist. But whatever your product is, try to make a wish list of people you'd like to 're-imagine' your brand. Just seeing it through their eyes could give you some new ideas.

DECISION POINT

You've opened up new roads for your idea so it can be developed or brought to a bigger audience. It's time to move on to the next stage. So, do you want to:

Make some fast cash   **p 255**

Get group feedback   **p 271**

STAGE 3: I'VE GOT TOO MANY MEETINGS

How you balance the main part of your business with the stuff you really want to do is hard. Especially once you've got a team on board, or your enterprise has grown. Sometimes people want you to be in on the detail or have you deal with the admin side of your business, which can be majorly annoying because it takes you away from doing all the creative stuff you love and want to do.

I knew I didn't just want to be a figurehead for SB.TV but I also didn't want to spend all my days in meetings, so I got other people involved who shared my vision but who could take care of that stuff. That meant hiring a shit-hot PA and having a lawyer and accountant, because I still wanna be out there filming sick people doing their thing. I'm still like 'Yessss,' when I've got a really good video to upload. So it's important to find a balance, because I can't always be filming stuff and I can't always be in meetings.

If you can't afford to hire people full-time you'll need to streamline the amount of time you spend in meetings. Here are some tips:

- **Have a time limit. No more than an hour per meeting, with a clear goal set out at the beginning, and a plan for who's going to put your decisions into action at the end. Don't forget to follow up that plan a few days later.**
- **Block out time in your diary where no one is allowed to put in meetings. Be firm and don't ever plan**

meetings at that time. If people know you're persuadable, they'll try and persuade you again.

- Sit with your team, not in an office. That way you can make decisions on the fly, rather than having to bat emails back and forth or have meetings about them.

- Start each week with a team meeting, where everyone signs up to what they're going to get done each day. Doing this publicly makes everybody accountable for their own work.

- Try to call people when you can, rather than emailing all the time – it can make things quicker and it's easy to miss an email when your inbox has loads of messages in it.

Once you've tried those and freed your time up a bit, I'm gonna send you back to the Decision Point on **p 257** (if you came from Make Some Fast Cash) or **p 266** (if you came from Check In with the Competition) so you can carry on with your journey.

STAGE 2: **MAKE SOME FAST CASH**

Obviously the ideal thing is to have a low-overhead business where it doesn't cost you very much to produce what you sell, so you can make the most profit. But if you're in a creative field, it can be harder to make money because it's really competitive and a lot of people expect art or entertainment to be free.

I'm not really motivated by money because music and broadcasting is my life. I still get a buzz from uploading videos and seeing the response they get. Also I've seen people make a load of money and then just blow it on the same stuff they always have, but more expensive versions. This seems kind of pointless to me, which is probably why most of my money gets spent on baseball caps and food. As you know, I've got a bit of a Thomas Sabo jewellery obsession, but that's pretty much my only guilty pleasure :)

However, there are always going to be times when you need a bit of extra cash fast, to make an idea happen. To do this, you're going to need to forget who you are a little bit, because this is all about doing whatever it takes to make money, regardless of what you're interested in.

Sometimes, when you get so focused on what you're doing and what you're trying to achieve, you don't necessarily notice other opportunities that are staring you in the face. Concentrating on your goals is important, but it's like that saying: sometimes you don't see the wood for the trees. So take a step back and get the full picture.

See opportunities in everything

For this task, I want you to think about profit in the same kind of obvious, simple way. Go into town and analyse it like a robot or human calculator. What's selling? What do you think the profit margin is on those items? What is there a craze for right at this minute? Have a walk around and make a mental, or physical, note of what you see. Because you're going to choose something to sell that will make you money quickly, something that you know there's already a demand for.

This is what most old-style entrepreneurs would do. They look at the world in a really pure, basic way, and work out what products have the biggest market – so maybe it's drinks dispenser machines in gyms, because everyone gets thirsty after working out. Or maybe they'll look at lunchtime food, because nearly everyone buys their lunch rather than makes it. That's the kind of thinking you need to adopt. Or it might just be flipping things – buying stuff that's limited and flipping it on eBay.

Obviously the other thing you need to do if you want to make money fast is to make sure your 'shop' is cheap to run. So either look at sites like Etsy, eBay and Big Cartel, or find a cheap place to get a market stall.

The only thing you're not allowed to do at this stage is have too much ego – you can't look down your nose at stuff. The minute you do that you'll miss loads of opportunities. If you're sure in yourself and you know why you're doing this (to fund your vision, which is much more important), you won't care about any of that stuff.

The thing I always remember about making money in this way is that you see it on reality telly all the time – those TV programmes where people are given £100 and a day to turn it into more money. You're not on telly, but you need to put yourself under pressure in the same sort of way, because you'll really surprise yourself. It might even turn into a neat little sideline that helps you fund your business.

I wanna hear from you if you made some money to fund your vision, so tweet me @selfbelievers and let me know what happened. Nothing shady!! And then it's time to make a choice. How's it going?

DECISION POINT

Now you've done that, it's time to take a look at another way to 'Keep It Fresh'. What's on your mind as you head into Stage 3?

I've got too many meetings   p 253

I wanna celebrate my success!   p 267

STAGE 1: I WANT A HOLIDAY

Aw man, are you tired? C'mon! Seriously though, it's OK, because sometimes you have to rest up, before you can fix up. If you need permission from me to take a day off – here, it's yours. Sort yourself out, go home, be with your family, chill out, play some PlayStation, do what you need to do to take your mind off things.

If you're making any kind of money for yourself at all, you need to recognise and give yourself credit because that's an amazing achievement. If you're already doing your own thing – no matter how hard it is or how tired you are – you're already winning.

When you make yourself a figurehead for your business, or if you've followed my advice about integrating your story into your brand, it can feel like a whole load of pressure. That's another way young modern entrepreneurs are different – they put so much of themselves into the brands they create – there's none of that, 'It's just business, it's not personal.' It's TOTALLY personal. So, of course, they take it to heart when their brand is attacked or things don't go well.

What you have to remember is that all the energy we put out into the world turns into something – whether it's making new connections, putting new skills into practice or just supporting what other people are doing. That can take it out of you, so it's OK to take a holiday. But stay conscious – don't just go back to work and do things exactly the same way if it's been making you stressed. Sit down at the end of your holiday and work out how you're going to do things better when you get back – whether it's partying less or working out more.

Good. You've had a rest, thought about what you can do to make your life less stressful, so you're ready to go back to the Decision Point on **p 249** and take action.

EnD OF LEUEL 6: OH MY DAYS IT WAS BAD

You've MADE IT!

OK, take a deep breath!! If you feel like this has all just been a massive stress, it's time to chill out. If you've read this level, you'll have seen that I made TONS of mistakes along the way – I nearly gave away 50 per cent of my company at one point! You're not alone, you *did* something. And maybe it didn't turn out perfect, but that's cool.

What *is* different about you is that you *tried*. I know that sounds like something teachers or your mum would say, but it's true. So many people aren't brave enough to do what you've done, to put themselves on the line and tell the world that they have an idea they believe in. You had the guts to do that, and it's something you should be really proud of.

You probably know what I'm gonna say now, but I wouldn't recommend this if I didn't do it myself. You need to reflect and work out why things didn't go as well as you expected. This is sometimes hard to do because you have to look your idea in the face and be prepared to admit you didn't think it through. But it's not about being hard on yourself or blaming yourself. Sometimes ideas need to happen at the right time, so maybe your timing was off. That's not necessarily something you could have done anything about.

The best thing about recognising when things aren't right is that it means you're opening another door, the one to your future, where another idea pushes you forward. Keep going, and whatever you do, believe in yourself.

You've come a long way and you need to hold on to that.

And remember, the only person who's gonna stop you doing what you want to do is you. So take some time out, and let's go back to the beginning on **p 237** and work through this level again to see if you can figure out where you're getting hung up. Your journey's never over and this is just a bump in the road.

Come on, we're in this together – let's take it back to the start.

STAGE 3: I WANNA GIVE BACK

Back to school

One of the ways I keep things fresh at SB.TV is finding ways to give back. It was funny – when I went back to Acton High School, some of the teachers who I thought hated me were proud that I'd done so well. They were all saying, 'Oh, I used to teach Jamal!' It made them look cool, too. It was jokes though, because some of the kids asked the teachers, 'Did you know this was gonna happen to Jamal? Could you tell he was gonna be a success?' and they were like, 'Yeah, we did!' – even though they tried to kick me out! And if they *had* kicked me out of school, I don't think SB.TV would have happened.

Whatever your teachers said about you then, you're doing great stuff now, and you're in the best position to inspire other young people to be confident enough to follow their dream. They're more likely to listen to you than when you were starting out. I like to tell kids in school my story, but I always make sure they don't just have me there to give a talk. Because I remember being their age and how much I hated it when people came in and talked to us for hours, without asking us what we thought. I like it to be a two-way thing, so I always ask for it to be a Q&A.

Reach into your wallet

SB.TV works with loads of charities now. If you're in a place to be able to give back financially then do it. It isn't *totally* selfless (though we'd give to charity regardless) because we are not a faceless organisation and we make it clear we care through charitable work, so the charity benefits and so does SB.TV.

You'll know when you're ready to work with charities, because you'll want to do it right, and give them the time and skills they deserve. You don't want to skimp on that. And when you're ready, it's important to choose a charity that you really care about, which campaigns on issues that are close to your heart.

SB.TV works with organisations like The Prince's Trust, MTV, HIV Staying Alive Foundation and Spirit of London awards, and I chose them because they're all charities that work on issues that affect young people. With Staying Alive Foundation, I was just moved by the stories of people who had stigma around them because of being affected by HIV. The Spirit of London awards reward young people who are doing things in their community. I never really had award schemes like that when I was starting out, so I like the idea of helping other young people move up. You should always bring people up with you.

The other thing to remember is that if you can't commit to an ongoing project with a charity, you can still do a one-off event. Find a local charity in your home town, invite them to meet with you, and then brainstorm a project you can work on – whether it's donating part of the profits from a limited-edition range of products you make, or a one-off talk or workshop, or giving them a percentage of your profits on a particular day. You'll be able to raise the profile of their charity through your social media channels, you might be able to get some press out of it, and you can put their logo on your website. Again, this is win-win.

DECISION POINT

This is kind of mad, but we're now nearly at the end of *Self Belief: The Vision.* I've got a few last words for you so, depending on how you're feeling, pick one of the following:

Boom! Success   p 274

OK, but I might need to try again   p 280

Oh my days it was bad   p 260

STAGE 2: **CHECK IN WITH THE COMPETITION**

I always say, 'Chase your dreams, not the competition' because I think it's so important that people focus on what they're doing rather than getting worked up about what everyone else is doing. This can happen a lot when you're young because young people are really vocal: they tell you when they like something, they have loads of opinions and they feel really strongly about things. This is great if your business or idea is aimed at young people because you can find out really quickly how it's being received by them – market research just kind of happens.

But sometimes you're *too* aware of what everyone else thinks, to the point that you can get a bit paranoid when you try out something new, because you're worried everyone's gonna shoot you down. It's terrible if this kind of paranoia stops you from doing things you believe in, because you have to have faith that your instincts are good, and that if you're proud of something, it's OK to shout about it. That can be a tricky balance.

Saying that, there *are* times when you do need to know what your competitors are doing, simply in terms of the experience they're giving their audience or customers. And now might be a good time to do that – to find out what would happen if you were a customer and you interacted with your competitor. What happens when you email them with a complaint? What happens when you ring them to get a quote? This can give you loads of useful information that they would never normally let you see; normally it would be secret. But if you ring them yourself, you can find out how they do what they do, so you can be sure to offer something much, much better.

Time to step into enemy territory ;)

The first thing you'll need to do is decide whether you want to try out their service (buy their product) or just interact with them on say, Twitter. Set up a new email address or call them from someone else's phone if necessary, and contact them to get a quote or ask questions, as if you were a potential customer. Get a couple of people to do it (not so many that it looks suspicious) and pull all your results together.

You're already at a stage in your vision where it's good to look back. Interacting with your competitors will do one of two things: it'll either make you realise you need to up your game, or you'll come away feeling proud that your service is better than your competitor's.

Either result will help your business.

DECISION POINT

Now you've done that, it's time to take a look at another way to 'Keep It Fresh'. What's on your mind as you head into Stage 3?

I've got too many meetings   p 253

I wanna celebrate my success!   p 267

STAGE 3: I WANNA CELEBRATE MY SUCCESS!

Haha, yeah you do! If your idea has been successful, OK, it might be time to celebrate. I never really need an excuse to go out raving. But there's raving, and there's *raving with purpose.*

From a business point of view, a party is a great thing because you can get your whole team together, bond and have fun. But you should also invite all the people who've helped you along the way, because that's when it's not only fun, it's useful; it's an opportunity. Parties are a great way of getting publicity and feedback – especially if you're re-launching your website or have a new product line. They also don't need to cost loads of money if you're smart about organising them.

Party with a purpose

When you did Level 4, you'll know that you need a purpose for your party. What's it for? It SHOULD be about how your idea's grown and how you've all worked together to make it happen. So make it relevant. Try these ideas on for size...

- Show some footage of your story so far – photos, videos, whatever (these are great things to have, even if you're not an online business). Parties are a great time to show things like this because you'll get immediate feedback. Think of it as a highlights reel – no more than five minutes, but you might be able to persuade a student at an art college or on a media course to make one for you. (You could agree to put their URL on the end if you don't have much budget.)

- If you show this at the party, it'll do two things. One: it's a good way for you and your team to reflect on your journey, which should raise everyone's spirits. Two: it'll force you to edit down the story of your brand, so it's absolutely clear what you're offering your customers. If you started out scribbling on bus tickets and ended up with a T-shirt business, your showreel should tell that story. This is another reason why you should try to document your journey along the way and KEEP EVERYTHING.

- Get up and talk to the people at your party about a new direction you're taking – whether it's a service, product or limited-edition range. Don't be afraid to do this. If you're inviting people for drinks, they won't mind you doing a quick speech. Remember to give people something to take away – whether it's a goodie bag that might persuade them to come in the first place, or just a card with all your web details on it.

- Basically, don't waste the opportunity of having all those contacts in one room. You should talk to as many people as you can, either to tell them about what you're doing, or thank them for helping you. Don't be scared, because they wouldn't have come if they weren't interested in you.

Whatever you do don't go crazy and blow your money on this. There are loads of ways to keep it cheap.

- Think about asking a small, new food company to get on board and provide the catering. You can let them put up banners/flyers or offer to give them some of your contacts in return for doing this.

- You've got nothing to lose by ringing a few drinks companies to see if they want to sponsor your event.
- If you're getting a good rep in whatever it is you're doing, you have power, so you can always do a deal by offering free banner ads on your website or letting a drinks company sponsor your monthly email mail-out.

Think creatively and remember that you've got absolutely nothing to lose in asking. You need this party to be as cheap as possible (us Brits like to drink), so be smart and see if you can do deals on everything, including the venue, food, drinks and DJ.

People to invite:

- your team (obviously)
- anyone you work with – clients, lawyers, accountants, managers
- anyone with power in your industry
- mentors
- work-experience people
- journalists
- bloggers

You should also think quite broadly and invite people you don't know. If there's someone on your wish list who you would love to work with, send them a personal email explaining why they mean something to you, and how much you want them to come. People respond to flattery – even more so if it's genuine!

DECISION POINT

I can't believe it, but we're near the end of the last level of *Self Belief: The Vision*. I'm buzzing!! But how are *you* feeling?

Boom! Success	p 274
OK, but I might need to try again	p 280
Oh my days it was bad	p 260

STAGE 2: **GET GROUP FEEDBACK**

As long as you have new ideas, you'll always be on top of your game. Some people think you only have a limited amount of time in the spotlight before your turn is over, but I don't worry about that. It's much better to spend your time thinking up *new* things you could do with your life than worrying about keeping hold of what you have. I've expanded SB.TV into doing loads of other channels, but that doesn't mean we've diluted our vision. Because now there'll be more opportunities if, like, a company want to do a tie-in with the SB.TV Fashion channel, or do a video for SB.TV Games & Gadgets. It's good to keep moving. I've opened my horizons a lot more, to let more people in on what I'm doing. You rest, you rust.

The only problem is that the more successful you are, the greater the risk. You've got further to fall. But being an entrepreneur is all about branching out and not being afraid of the future, even if there's a recession, and even if your business is worth a lot of money. You might get a load of people panicking that if you do try a new venture, it's all going to go wrong. You might fail; people's jobs might be at risk.

I'm not saying this is easy stuff to get your head around, and I'm not saying you should just disappear and make huge changes, especially if they're going to affect your team. But to come up with your best ideas you need to be in a positive frame of mind, amongst people who believe in you, who aren't afraid. Get away from your computer, get away from your office, get your team out in a park or something, be somewhere you can think freely. Get back in The Bubble (remember Level 1?), don't get distracted.

Then you need to Focus Group it – to run it past your audience. Not people who've been in your industry for years and who might be a bit bitter, but your actual consumers, the people who buy or use your product. Get out on the street, talk to your people, even if that means stopping mums in the shops or going down to a local college to talk to students. Market research is vital and it's free, if you can take the time out to do it. Get some real feedback from real people. Feed that back into your new idea.

Then you need to run it past some more cautious people. The weird thing is, people who see risk everywhere can be useful because they might point out stuff that you haven't considered. You'll be able to tell if their criticism comes from a place of jealousy or fear – usually it's obvious – so don't let it bring you down. Be practical, not emotional, about it.

Then go back to your team with all opinions fed in, and work out a way to trial your idea. Remember that you don't need to do a full-scale launch of your idea, because that'll cost you a load of money and you don't yet know if it works. Like we did in the earlier levels, you can always find a way to do a dummy run that is less risky, like in Level 4, and you should do that now. If it works, great. If it doesn't, move on, do another brainstorm.

Through all this it's important to recognise that you're never going to be perfect. If this book is about anything, it's about starting a journey and then realising that the journey is endless. It will go on as long as you have energy to do it. Like me, I don't think I'm ever going to reach a point where I say I'm done, or that I've made it.

This isn't how you have to be, but I don't think I'll ever reach a point where I'll say, 'Yes. This is success.' So always try to think, 'Right, what's the next thing?' Look at Richard Branson. He's going to SPACE! People say he should retire with the amount of money he's got, but he shows me, like 'How *dare* I say I've made it? How CAN I say I've made it?' Focus groups help you work out which ideas will keep you and your customers/supporters excited.

DECISION POINT

Promise me you won't skip on the stuff I suggest doing in all the levels. If you don't try some of the tasks suggested you're not gonna get the full benefit of *Self Belief: The Vision*. And I REALLY want you to get as much as you can out of this whole process.

So, it's time to make a choice again. Where's your head at?

I wanna give back   **p 262**

It's all a blur   **p 278**

END OF LEVEL 6: **BOOM! SUCCESS**

If you've chosen this option I want to hear from you. I mean, I want to hear from *everyone* but I get a buzz when someone is happy about what they're doing. The energy I get off that is infectious, it helps me do what I do. So if you've finished this book on a high I am so happy for you, that's amazing. Tweet me @selfbelievers!

Through starting SB.TV I've been able to do so many awesome things, I feel blessed for life. I could stop now and feel happy – even though I feel like I'll never stop, because there's too much out there. The motivation for me is still making videos. I think it's sick that I can make one and know that loads of people are going to see it and talk about it. I love that feeling, I love breaking fresh talent and I really love the idea that there are loads of people checking SB.TV every day when they get home from school. To know that I've done that gives me a buzz. That's sick. That's worth way much more than money to me, that the videos I shoot are being watched by people, and that SB.TV is why people come up and ask me for a picture.

If you're feeling even one per cent of that after doing these levels, you can imagine how good you're going to feel in two years. Or five, or ten. Take a second now, and expect the unexpected, dream a bit of what's ahead. Because, hopefully, you've changed your own life in reading *Self Belief: The Vision*, and it's just going to get better. Good luck.

Depending which paths you took through this level, you might want to go back to the start and choose another route, to try different tasks and find more *Self Belief: The Vision* ideas. All you need to do is go to **p 237** and we'll go back and check out other ways to keep things fresh.

STAGE 2: GET MORE TIME FOR ME

When you're running your own business or trying to see through your own idea, you've got to remember to take time out. If you've done all the tasks I've set you so far, you'll have been busy, so maybe your friends haven't seen you for a while. But it's important not to feel like you're chained to your laptop or that you're in your office, studio or workshop 24/7, so you need to schedule breaks. If I'm getting stressed it doesn't take me long to get back on track, because I just chill out, enter The Bubble and play some PlayStation with my mates. You need to do this often just to get your head straight. (If you need a reminder about The Bubble, have a look back at Level 1.)

This is most important if you're working from home, because if you work from home, your work *is* your life. It can send you crazy, you can get obsessive. And that's no good if you want to keep coming up with good ideas. You need to be fresh on it.

- The easiest way to keep things compartmentalised in your brain is to keep fairly regular hours – so you sit down wherever you work at 9 a.m. or 10 a.m. and then clock off at 5 p.m. or 6 p.m. There's gonna be times when that's not realistic, but that's OK. Just don't be a dummy and do things like working while sitting on your bed until late, because you need to keep some spaces clear for chilling.
- You can always go and work in a library or cafe if you really want to separate your work life from your home – even if you only do your emails and admin there.

- You also need to turn off your work emails at home every now and then, or you'll still be reading them in bed at 1 a.m. and you won't be able to sleep.
- Make sure people on your team are confident in what they're doing, so you're not the only person people can call if there's a problem.
- Choose someone in your team to handle day-to-day enquiries so you don't get called about the tiny stuff, but make sure you *are* called when your brand is in trouble. If you're the boss, it's up to you to make sure this chain of command is in place and that it works properly. You can't blame your team for calling you all the time if you didn't tell them any different.

The other way to stop getting all obsessive is to ban yourself from ego-surfing. I Google myself every now and then, and check the news and the blogs because it's good to have a look, but don't make a habit of it. I used to do it all the time but now I just allow people to say what they say and I let them get on with it. I also don't have Google alerts set up. But a smart thing can be to make sure someone else does – so they can act as a filter for any bad press you're getting and then only forward it on if it's something you need to worry about. Then you won't have to plough through a load of nonsense.

DECISION POINT

Promise me you won't skip on the stuff I suggest doing in all the levels. If you don't try some of the tasks suggested you're not gonna get the full benefit of *Self Belief: The Vision*. And I REALLY want you to get as much as you can out of this whole process.

So, it's time to make a choice again. Where's your head at?

I wanna give back p 262
It's all a blur p 278

STAGE 3: IT'S ALL A BLUR

If you picked this option, I know how you feel. Sometimes I can barely remember what happened last week, never mind two years ago. It can feel like a blur, like time has just gone, and you don't know where.

When you're crazy busy it's hard, but there's only one way to slow things down. Being organised. o_o I know. If you're a creative person you'll find it hard, but here are a couple of things I learned and wished I'd known earlier...

Keep track of your money

One thing I wish I'd known before I got started with SB.TV is that you should keep your receipts. I just wish someone had told me, 'Whatever you do, keep receipts for EVERYTHING!' I mean, my Mum told me to do that a couple of times when I was younger, but if I'd had it drilled into me like my maths times tables, then I'd be a lot better off! It means you can keep an eye on what you're spending so you don't go mental, and you can keep a check on whether you've paid bills and stuff, so you don't get hit with a fine or worse.

Archive your work

I really wish someone had told me never to tape over a video without making a copy. My mum kept a book of all her newspaper cuttings in her music career, and I wish I had a book like that. Some of the videos I first made for YouTube are gone forever. I probably shouldn't admit that, but it's true. And I wish I'd saved them. I even recorded over some interviews we did. I mean, I recorded over Kelly Rowland! Obviously I already had the video uploaded to YouTube, and I did it because I couldn't afford to buy new tapes at the time, but I didn't have a back-up, so when I got more successful, people were horrified that I was working in that way. I really regret that, but it's OK to get it wrong. As long as you recognise it, and change how you work.

That's kind of the key to slowing down time – it's keeping track of what you've done, and taking time to look back and be proud of what you've achieved. Whatever it was, make a promise to yourself now that you'll keep those souvenirs from your past, however rubbish they seem, so you can look back at your journey when times are rough.

Now you've learned how to stop time o_o!! Let's go back to the Decision Point on **p 273** (if you came from Get Group Feedback) or **p 277** (if you came from Get More Time for Me) and take another option now you're in control.

END OF LEVEL 6: OK, BUT I MIGHT NEED TO TRY AGAIN

Listen, staying grounded is the number one most important thing. So if you're feeling like you've only part succeeded, don't beat yourself up about it. Recognising your mistakes and still having the courage to carry on is exactly what makes a good entrepreneur great. It's what makes you stand apart from the people around you as someone who can keep trying and stay humble. You've got to remember that no path to the top is without its hard times; you're going to hit difficulties whatever you do.

It sounds like you still want to change some things and work on yourself, which is great. The first thing you should do is go out and have some fun. Because you've been working hard, you probably need a break to clear your mind and recharge.

After you've done that, get out of the house, college or office, and go somewhere you really love, have a drink, and think about what things you need to work on. The whole point of these levels in *Self Belief: The Vision* is that they're designed to be repeated and played more than once. So you're not likely to feel like you're perfect already, are you?

Right, now you've had a break and a breather, see how you feel. It might be time for you to head back to the start of Level 6 and take yourself through some more options, try some more tasks and make sure you're feeling confident. If that's the case, we'll go back to the beginning on **p 237** together.

If you think you've pretty much got the tools to go on and have bigger and better success, then that's awesome. Thanks for joining me on these levels, and hit me up on Twitter @selfbelievers to tell me all about it!

STAGE 1: I FEEL LIKE A SELL-OUT

When you start to become successful you'll be criticised, whatever you do and however you do it. I'm no different. I get dissed for not being able to film everybody who wants a video on SB.TV. I know I'm working hard and I do as much as I can, but if I wasn't so confident in my vision or so sure of where we're going, it would mess me up. I could take it all personally, but you can't please everyone. And if you tried to, it's likely your vision would end up weak.

If you feel like a 'sell-out' then maybe you're just saying you're not sure about some of the decisions you've made. Maybe you did a deal with someone who compromised your vision. Or maybe you worked with some people who weren't as cool as they first seemed. Whatever happened, it's important to work out where you got this idea – did other people call you a sell-out? Or do you need to take responsibility for a decision you're not proud of? You need to work out first if this 'selling out' idea comes from you or someone else.

On the way to a meeting in a taxi once we stopped at some traffic lights and I saw this young guy in the park, and then I saw him look over and recognise me. He had one of those tunics on because he was working for a charity, like where they ask you to sign up in the street to donate money. Then this weird thing happened, because I saw him hide from me, as if he was embarrassed about what he was doing, embarrassed about his job. He'd got pride, so after he saw me, he kind of hid behind a tree so I couldn't see him.

I hated it, because no one should feel ashamed of their job, whatever it is. All jobs are important, and whether you're doing something just to get by, to help you get to where you want to be, or if you are doing something you love but think other people will laugh at it, you shouldn't feel embarrassed by what you do. Don't let anyone – including yourself – make you feel bad. Regardless of what you're doing, you should be proud of your work.

Sometimes I feel the perception of me is that I went from the 266 bus to going around in a private jet and it's totally out of proportion. And maybe some people think I'm just in it for that kind of thing. It's important that people know I don't spend my money on stupid stuff like that. It's not all about cars and money. It's funny because if I then decide to get the bus, people will ask me why. And then I'm like 'Why would you not get the bus, it's the easiest way to get around?'

What I'm saying is that in any given situation there are a thousand different possibilities for what's really happening. Some people might see me in a flash car and think I've sold out, or that I only care about money. And that guy in the park thought I would judge him for some reason. You can't worry about this stuff because you can't control it. The only thing you can do is be humble and trust your inner critic. You can only judge yourself.

What's making you feel like this?

That's why it's important to work out if this idea about 'selling out' comes from you or from the outside. If it's you, then you need to deal with any mistakes you made so you can restore your pride. If it comes from other people, forget it. If you're doing what you need to do and you're not hurting other people, be proud of it.

The other way of addressing this is to think about where you've come from, or take some time to reconnect with your roots. I go back to the ends not just because I love Acton and

Luton but because that restores me, it helps me feel like Jamal Edwards again. It helps me remember the kid I was at fifteen starting out. Hopefully one day I'll really be able to give something back to the area where I grew up – whether it's building a sick youth club, or a community hall or something.

I'm from an area where it's not always easy to do the right thing. When I go back it means a lot to have people come up to me and show me love when they don't have to and say they respect me, because it makes me want to work harder. It's pressure, but I want to show them what's possible. And then when they see me with Dr Dre in Asia, they can say, 'He's from where we are, and he's done it'. It shows what I've got is reachable, because I was in the same place as all those people. So I always go there and show my face and show I'm still about.

DECISION POINT

You've gone back to your roots and got back a feeling that you're doing something worthwhile, and you've not turned into a money machine. It's a really good thing to keep checking in with yourself – it's easy to lose your way when you're so far from where you started out.

But now it's time to head on to stage 2 of *Keep It Fresh*. So what are you ready to do next?

Check in with the competition　　　　　**p 265**

Get more time for me　　　　　**p 275**

ACKNOWLEDGEMENTS

First off, I'd like to thank my beloved mum, dad and sister for standing by me throughout: you guys are my rock, my inspiration and the motivation for me to achieve my goals. I genuinely believe a happy home makes a happy soul. Thank you for your patience while I've been preoccupied with even more new ventures, which cut down on the precious time I can spend with you. I have nothing but love and admiration for you.

Team SB – past and present – you are my heart. Your diverse opinions, unique creative talents, energy for the digital space and consistent support and hard work has helped me, not only to develop the business but to provide a clear vision that's also shaped me as a man. You all are SB.TV as much as I am. I love you and this would not be possible without you all. A big thank you (in alphabetical order) to the team who've helped SB.TV grow: Georgia Anderson, Aaron Bridgeman, Saskia Collins, James Hanna, Natalia Jorquera, Morgan Kisch, Lewis Knaggs, Lily Mercer, Hass Mosa, Lance Penez, James Rees, Rick Tank, Liam Tootill, Ricky Williams, Becca Wren and Paris Zarcilla for the work you do on a daily basis as SB.TV continues to expand. I know it can get a little hectic at times but I guess that's what being young is all about. Here's to the future too :-)

I owe a huge thanks to the amazing people who provided forewords for this book (in the order they appear in the levels of *Self Belief: The Vision*): Sir Richard Branson, Jack and Finn Harries, Emeli Sandé, Ed Sheeran, Jessie J and Idris Elba. I'm so blessed to be able to call you my friends. I still cannot believe I have you all in my life. Thank you for all of your continued kind and generous remarks.

So much gratitude to Tony Hingerton – I may not have known him for the longest time, but I still class him as one of my best mates. He kept it real with me and we have been on some mad raving missions, haha. Love, bro!

I wholeheartedly appreciate Isaac Densu – my oracle. This guy just talks a lot, haha. Keep talking though, bro. I am appreciative for everything you've done and continue to do for me. Thank you for your integrity and virtuousness.

A major thank you to Tim Katoga – with so many ideas running through my head on a day-to-day basis, you help me turn them into coherent thoughts and words. Thank you, bro!

I'm indebted to the great qualities of Billy McCarthy, who is not only my friend, but has also helped me a lot by driving me around EVERYWHERE – we've had some long journeys on the way to film people. You've kept me safe as I've been on my travels. I miss and thank you for all those long, productive conversations that have inspired me.

Speaking of encouragement, I must mention that Roger Ames and Charlie Lycett have been responsible for being gurus in my life. Your assistance, guidance and support helped me evolve into the businessman I am today, and for that I thank you. Your enlightened and wise words of advice have been invaluable.

I'd also like to extend my appreciation to Richard Antwi, Alex Boateng and Marvyn Harrison, who were there in the beginning and helped me strike my first agency deal with YouTube, alongside many other things. I haven't forgotten! You are great people and I can only be grateful to have met and worked with you all.

A big shout out to my publishing team who've worked on the book: thank you (in alphabetical order) to Shona Abhyankar for your great PR tactics and congeniality; to Commissioning Editor Hannah Knowles, without you this book wouldn't have happened, and for that and all your hard work on this, I'm so thankful; to Crystal Mahey-Morgan, I am so grateful for your business expertise, creative thinking and dedication in putting together a sick strategy; to Gail Rebuck for also believing in the project; to Wendy Roby for knowing how to get the best out of me so others could get the most out of this book; and not forgetting the whole machine at Random House/ Virgin Books.

Furthermore, to every musician/artist/person that has appeared on SB.TV, thank you for sharing your talent and aptitude with me and the rest of the SB.TV audience.

Last, but definitely not least, I would like to offer a big thank you to all you supporters who have been with me from the start, whether that's been watching my videos or featuring on SB.TV. Thank you for everything you've ever done and continue to do for me and SB.TV, no matter how small. You truly do make my work worth doing. I hope my book inspires you to chase after your life goals and dreams. Remember, nothing is impossible.

Jamal Edwards